THE YEAR OF THE WOMBAT
ENGLAND: 1857

The Wombat. From J. Gould, *The Mammals of Australia*, 1855

Francis Watson

THE YEAR OF THE WOMBAT
ENGLAND: 1857

LONDON
VICTOR GOLLANCZ LTD
1974

Printed in Great Britain by
The Camelot Press Ltd, Southampton

ACKNOWLEDGEMENTS

FOR ASSISTANCE ON various points of enquiry I have to thank
Mr D. M. Archer of the Victoria and Albert Museum; Mr J. S.
Maas; Mr R. C. Mackworth-Young, Royal Librarian at Windsor
Castle; Miss M. E. Pillers, the Dickens House Curator; and Sir
Charles Tennyson.
Permission to quote from letters and diaries has been accorded
by Mrs Cecil Woodham Smith and Messrs Constable (*Florence
Nightingale*), and by Messrs Jonathan Cape and the editor Edgar
Johnson (*Letters of Charles Dickens to the Baroness Burdett-Coutts*).
Acknowledgement in the latter case is also made to the Meredith
Press, New York.
The photograph of the Royal Family at Osborne has been
reproduced by gracious permission of Her Majesty the Queen,
and that of Carlyle in his garden by courtesy of the National
Trust. Sir Richard Proby has kindly allowed me to include a
reproduction of O'Neil's painting *Eastward Ho!* from his collection at Elton Hall, Peterborough. Permission in respect of Morris's
copy of FitzGerald's *Rubaiyat*, of Rossetti's self-portrait with the
dead wombat, and of the 1857 *Keepsake*, has been given by the
Trustees of the British Museum; and by the London Museum
Trustees for Ritchie's *Summer Day in Hyde Park* and Levin's
Dancing-Platform at Cremorne. Rossetti's portrait of Miss Siddal,
and the photographs of the Crystal Palace and of I. K. Brunel,
are acknowledged to the Victoria and Albert Museum, Crown
Copyright. Wallis's *Chatterton*, Rossetti's *Wedding of St George*, and
Dadd's *Fairy-Feller's Masterstroke* are reproduced by consent of
the Trustees of the Tate Gallery, London; the portraits of Ruskin
and Miss Nightingale by that of the Trustees of the National
Portrait Gallery. Rossetti's drawings of Guinevere and of St
Cecilia are from the City of Birmingham Museum and Art
Gallery, and the portrait of Dickens from the Dickens House,
Doughty Street, London. Dodgson's photograph of Tennyson
is in the Tennyson Research Centre, Lincoln, and is reproduced
by kind permission of the Director, City of Lincoln Libraries,

Museum and Art Gallery. All other illustrations, with the exception of the frontispiece and the Crim-Con Meter, have been supplied by the Mansell Collection.

F. W.

CONTENTS

LIST OF ILLUSTRATIONS

I

PRELUDE
The Hollow and Fantastical

THE WOMBAT'S LAIR, as it came to be called within the circle charmed by Dante Gabriel Rossetti, was a place of assignation. The casual visitor to the Zoological Society's collection in Regent's Park might easily miss it, though the clue was in the official guidebook: "A portion of the *Porcupine Inclosure* is appropriated to a pair of very singular Marsupial Animals from Tasmania, which, for the first time on record, bred here in the spring of 1856." Perhaps the little family that lodged with the porcupines seldom emerged together from their burrow. At all events it was a generic individuality that called for recognition: not *a* wombat but The Wombat, a droll and fubsy creature that by 1857, when Rossetti was twenty-nine, had him in its pocket.

The curious in this matter may be referred in the first instance to Mr Michael Archer's essay on *Rossetti and the Wombat* in the March, 1965, issue of *Apollo*, where the theme is carried forward to the more affluent years of the Rossetti bestiary in Chelsea. But the two wombats that were added at one time and another to the menagerie of a studio haunted by remorse and loneliness were to lose some of their significance among its other occupants: the armadillos, the peacocks and owls, the salamanders, the racoon that raided the neighbours' fowl-houses and the Indian bull, with eyes like Janey Morris, which nevertheless had to be disposed of after chasing and treeing its master, whose lithe and Latin beauty was by then giving way to corpulence. The conspicuous year comes down to us as that of the earlier tryst in Regent's Park. The Year of the Wombat, thus particularised, is 1857.

This was the boisterous and ecstatic prime when for Edward Burne-Jones the London streets still glittered with the youthful rapture shared with William Morris: the rapture of acceptance by Rossetti, "the greatest man in Europe", and thus by Ruskin also, avuncular at thirty-eight and master of "the most persuasive oratory we had ever heard." That silver tongue was the more persuasive for blaming the generation-gap upon the old rather than the young, but it had not yet shifted its emphasis from aesthetic doctrine to social protest. In half a century London had tripled its population to two-and-a-half million, and Edward Mayhew was combing appalling labyrinths to document *London Labour and the London Poor*. But Burne-Jones, as Rossetti reciprocated, was "one of the nicest young fellows in—Dreamland." So the streets glittered in subsequent memory, "and it was always morning, and the air sweet and full of bells." Val Prinsep finally clinched the matter, treasuring over the years the gathering of artists ("They are all the least bit crazy," confided Ruskin) for the Oxford mural-splashing in the Long Vacation of 1857. Rossetti, in Prinsep's testimony, was "the planet around which we revolved . . . All beautiful women were 'stunners' with us. Wombats were the most beautiful of God's creatures."

Some affinity with Rossetti might have been discernible in the animal's natural habits which, one would be told, "are nocturnal, and in beautiful accord with its instinct." An early traveller to the Antipodes, after introducing his readers to "a squat, short-legged and rather inactive quadruped," had offered evidence to show that its mild and gentle disposition, reflected in a normally placid countenance, was not to be imposed upon. "It bites hard and becomes furious when provoked." The lessons that could be learned from the animal kingdom provided in the eighteen-fifties numerous contributions to the *Zoological Keepsake*, and the best of reasons for taking the children to the Society's Garden and Museum. And a further report on the wombat, though not directly confirmed, gave it some claim to serve as model to a robustly advancing nation on the threshold of unrevealed trials:

> The natives state that it sometimes indulges in a long ramble, and if a river should cross its course, quietly walks into the water and traverses the bottom of the stream until it reaches the other side.

What seems to have captivated Rossetti, however, was the animal's complacent oddity—beginning, as Whistler was later to reflect, with its comical name. It was a name upon which the zoologists, with *Phascolymus wombat*, sought vainly to improve: a name which Edward Lear might have been happy to invent, adding a fanciful sketch to assist the wombat in inventing itself.

Which done, it can assume in retrospect a wider function than that of easing sensibilities strained in pursuit of an Arthurian dream. Bumbling about on its fat little legs, a poltergeist in Camelot, the rotund and plushy wombat can be allowed to preside over a year of bizarre concatenations of events and characters, a surrealistic and serendipitous year, a year of straining at gnats and tilting at windmills, in which the unthinkable becomes the inevitable, the incredible must be inflated before it can be believed, and nearly everybody—not just the Rossetti circus—seems at radiant intervals the least bit crazy. All of which reveals an exceptional character when we turn to that marginal but indispensable work, the diary of Charles Greville, to find him looking back, on the first day of 1858, upon "a year of fine weather of which nobody can recollect the like. This nearly unbroken course of wonderful weather for about nine or ten months gives rise to many speculations as to its cause."

When a summer of such epic proportions beams upon the Island Race, almost anything can happen. Even so, it must be borne in mind that the Year of the Wombat was preceded, and therefore to some extent prepared for, by the Year of the Scapegoat. Whatever young Mr Holman Hunt may have hoped to convey when he set up his easel on the edge of the Dead Sea, his gun beside him and an awkwardly restive goat tethered in the foreground, the compulsive strangeness of the result had made it the picture of the year in the Royal Academy Exhibition of 1856.

> While the hills of the Crimea were white with tents of war and the fiercest passions of the nations of Europe burned in high funeral flames over their innumerable dead, one peaceful English tent was pitched beside a shipless sea; and the whole strength of an English heart spent in painting a weary goat, dying upon its salt sand.

So wrote Ruskin, treating the picture to a long notice of balanced praise and blame, but without perceiving the uncanny relevance of its theme. For the bleating of scapegoats had been loud in the land as the Crimean War lurched and lapsed to a conclusion at which, when the tabarded Heralds announced the peace in London, the crowds jeered.

Much had been expected of that ill-managed adventure. Ruskin himself had looked towards the Crimea "for confirmation

of all our greatness, trial of our strength, purging and punishment of our futilities." And although Tennyson might later
protest at being saddled with the opinions of his poetic characters,
no apology had been needed in 1855 for the last climactic stanzas
of *Maud*; for the manly decision that "it is better to fight for the
good than to rail at the ill"; and for the vision

> Of a land that has lost for a little her lust of gold,
> And love of a peace that was full of wrongs and shames,
> Horrible, hateful, monstrous, not to be told;
> And hail once more to the banner of battle unroll'd.

Futility could be ennobled for all time at Balaclava, but war
merely added its own scandals to the wrongs and shames of peace.
Frustrated philanthropists, aware that they were only scratching
the surface of a mounting problem of brutalised poverty, had
to be sharply reminded by *The Times* that "there is no one to blame
for this; it is the result of nature's simplest laws"—whereupon
Charles Dickens, gestating a new novel, decided to call it *Nobody's
Fault*; but changed the title to *Little Dorrit* just before the first
instalment appeared.

For the war itself there had been a Russian despot to vilify.
But the death of Czar Nicholas at the height of the conflict
allowed his son Alexander, as soon as his allied challengers had
withdrawn their forces, to invite their state delegations to see
him crowned in Moscow in a despotic splendour that betrayed
no strain of war upon his imperial resources. Rumour put the
Czar's expenditure on this occasion even higher than the estimate
by Earl Granville, the chief British representative, of one million
sterling: which itself stood at twenty times the cost of Queen
Victoria's coronation and four times the extravagant outlay for
King George IV. "No country in Europe," added the Earl,
reporting his impressions of Russia to the Queen, "will furnish
so fair a chance of success to Socialism." For the British disburse-
ment on the late hostilities the Greville Diary offers at the close
of 1865 the sanguine reflection that "after three years of expensive
war the balance-sheet exhibited such a state of wealth and pros-
perity as may well make us the envy of surrounding nations."

It was a different balance-sheet—a seventy-three per cent loss
by disease alone to eight Regiments in six months—that had
imposed upon Florence Nightingale, just before the Queen sent
for her to Balmoral in September, 1856, the private vow: "I

stand at the altar of the murdered men, and while I live I fight their cause." In the history of the British army it was not exceptional for God's wonders to be performed at a prodigal rate of human wastage. What had been new, and less than glorious, was to have the facts reported fully in *The Times* and rancorously raised at Westminster. As the first war to make use of the electric telegraph, which by this time linked London with Constantinople, the Crimean affair began the transformation of an event by the relative immediacy of its projection.

It was also the first war to be photographed. Another boundary had been drawn, delimiting the past that is properly explored by history from the region of spurious identity which we still inhabit. Only an inspired foreknowledge of the law that nothing exists until it has entered our consciousness by way of the parturient lens can adequately account for the pioneering efficiency of Roger Fenton. He it was who fruitfully conveyed to that scene of logistical shambles himself and his cumbrous camera, his tent and stoves and portable dark-room, his baths and cistern and supplies of plate glass, his chemicals and distilled water, his thirty-six chests of necessaries: a prodigious armament to bring against Holman Hunt and his goat in the struggle to capture the appearance of truth.

Having played his part in the Crimea, Mr Fenton returned to England to share with other masters of the new craft in the creation of a new being. Charles Darwin was still collecting from rock pools the slithering ammunition for an attack on the immutability of species. Samuel Smiles had completed among the engineers his pilot-study towards the evolutionary doctrine of Self-Help. From a cave in the Neander Thal, near Düsseldorf, the lonely vestiges had just been recovered of a human specimen whom some identified—rather than betray the biblical chronology —as "a rickety Mongolian Cossack." But all the time the shadows on the wall of Plato's cave were yielding in the contest for survival to a realistically photographed anthropoid in a realistically photographed environment.

"If I could leave one man behind me!" moaned the national heroine, daily expecting to fall out from her forced march. But by the beginning of 1857 things were getting into perspective: a suburban perspective of Alma Villas, Sebastopol Gardens and Inkerman Terrace, sheltering infant daughters with the brand-new name of Florence, and welcoming papas who made their homeward way through fog and sleet, fortified by a nip at the *Lord Palmerston* and protected by their Raglan capes. For a timely death ("of a broken heart," it was widely supposed) had released Lord Raglan from the roles of Commander-in-Chief and principal scapegoat. The survival of the preposterous Lord Cardigan, on the other hand, not only enabled a personal legend to destroy itself, but deferred until the 1890's the memorial of another useful garment: a muffled tribute, when one considers the blaze of gold and blue and scarlet that had completed the astonishment of the Russian gunners at Balaclava as Cardigan rode clean through them.

Meanwhile, what Englishmen could do to sustain their credibility was done. Clouds of pipe-smoke began to hover over domestic scenes that had known only the lingering aroma of a surreptitious cigar, and *Punch* prepared to give the Great Tobacco Question parity with The Great Crinoline Problem. Moustaches now luxuriated upon upper lips whose stiffness had seemed to be called in question. The vast authoritative beard, so snug a resting-place for *Two Owls and a Hen, Four Larks and a Wren*, took a little longer to establish itself. But the Poet Laureate's hairiness, though disliked by Mrs Tennyson, finally became a national monument. Jane Welsh Carlyle considered that her husband's new appearance was that of an escaped maniac. When Carlyle pointed out that it saved him half an hour's shaving every day, she retorted that instead of giving the time to *Frederick the Great* he wasted it in drifting about the house in Cheyne Row, "bemoaning what's amiss with the Universe."

The reddish-gold beard of Holman Hunt, that went so ravishingly with his violet eyes, was adopted during his travels in the infidel Near East, in order that "amongst those peculiarly addicted people"—as he told his friend Millais, "I shall look less like a boy and escape without attention." Charles Dickens had the demands of amateur theatricals as excuse for the new cult, and so did his young associate Wilkie Collins. Both beards became permanent. But Lord Palmerston carried through the Year of the Wombat, in grizzled splendour, the bushy side-whiskers and unconcealed chin of a formidable age, of the buried Great Duke, of Arnold of Rugby, of Victoria's persevering Albert.

Some called the Prime Minister Pam and some called him Cupid, and in the royal family he was sometimes Germanised into Pilgerstein. Vaulting into the highest office to salvage the national pride, his intense and skilful application to the game had surprisingly earned the Queen's approbation, the Garter, and a cordial note of good wishes from Windsor Castle for Christmas 1856. Surprisingly, since this was essentially the same Palmerston whom his sovereign had a few years earlier desired to see, if see him she must, in his grave; the same Palmerston whose diplomacy, hardly less than his morals, had come under suspicion when, as an overnight guest at the Castle, he had ruined an assignation with one of Her Majesty's ladies by tapping on the wrong bedroom-door; the same unpredictable, apparently frivolous Whig aristocrat whose almost Radical effrontery at the Foreign Office had cost him his job. The loud, staccato laugh that could unnerve European Chancelleries, or warn a London hostess that her evening was at its climax, was now familiar music. And the success of his own receptions, at his mansion in Piccadilly, was further secured by the genuine charm of Lady Palmerston and the quality of the *cuisine*. "Lord Palmerston," testified one of his bitterest opponents, "is redeemed from the last extremity of political degradation by his cook."

Less grudgingly, Greville found himself moving by the end of 1856 from "the greatest aversion and mistrust" for Palmerston to the conclusion that he was "the best minister we can have." Gladstone, however, never ceased to deplore what he took to be the old gentleman's complete lack of principle or conviction, and Bright wrote him down as a charlatan. "He's a humbug," confided Miss Nightingale (who got on rather well with him), adding the saving comment: "and he knows it." Dickens savaged him as the Glib Vizier or Twirling Weathercock. Karl Marx called him "the old comic." Disraeli dismissed him as "that painted pantaloon." But not permanently. Forty years later, with the slightest creaking of his still fashionable stays, Disraeli bowed to the distant shade: "The two most manly persons I ever knew, Palmerston and Lyndhurst, both rouged. So one must not trust too much to general observations."

In the case of Lyndhurst, who also had his place in the 1857 revels, particular observations are harder to come by. Believing that "the life which requires a biographer has been insufficiently lived," he burned every letter and paper that he thought could be useful: which did not save him either from the customary two-volume tumulus, nor yet from certain snide attentions by

B

Lord Campbell, another luminary of 1857 whose *Lives of the Lord Chancellors of England* were said to have added a new sting to death. It is enough at this point to introduce the first and last Baron Lyndhurst as John Singleton Copley, son of the American painter (and himself in youth a student under Reynolds); and to mark the milestones of a shining legal-political career: the trial of Queen Caroline, Government office as Attorney-General, three separate terms as Lord Chancellor, and then the long autumn of an elder statesman. His sarcophagus of rosy granite in the upper wilderness of Highgate cemetery, at a decent remove from the magnetic shrine of Marx, has no epitaph. But Sir Henry Holland could have supplied it; "Lord Lyndhurst had all the virtues, and but one failing—a too keen perception of what is hollow and fantastical in human affairs."

This engaging weakness was shared in some degree by Palmerston, and perhaps rather more so by Disraeli. For 1857, when Lyndhurst was eighty-five, Palmerston seventy-three, and Disraeli fifty-three, such a perception was essential equipment. It was useful also to be able to forget 1856, the year which so many had spent in trying to forget what they could not atone for in 1855 and 1854. The reaction was understandable, and so was Florence Nightingale's despair. "We don't want to know any more," she fumed at Christmas 1856, "about the trenches cold and damp, the starved and frozen camp, the deficient rations, the stores which might have served the great army of the dead lying unused." The Queen herself took leave of 1856 as "this gloomy year." But she was carrying her ninth child, and pregnancy was so depressive to her nerves and spirits that Sir James Clark had given private warning, as her medical attendant, of the probability that she would "sink" under it. It was her mental constitution that perturbed him, as it perturbed her husband, watchful for any symptom of the Hanoverian malady.

Whatever may be feared and hoped for the Year of the Wombat, it is the scarcely precedented blaze of full-leafed summer that is least imaginable, as the curtains are drawn against the winter twilight and the table-tapping and the tea-leaf-scanning begin at the fireside. Or is that what has kindled the prescience of Dr Cumming to warn us of a comet for June of 1857, hesitating only as to whether it will strike the earth into instant, total and merited destruction, or simply cleanse it with the scorching temperatures of a near miss?

As a fundamentalist minister of London's Scottish Church, Dr Cumming might have regarded the death of Pope Urban IV in 1264, which had been associated with the comet's first recorded appearance, as an appropriate visitation. But the specialised expectations of astronomers served only as corroboration for the moral and scriptural certainty of cosmic catastrophe, which he had set forth in trenchant sermons and publications. For a second identification in 1556, religious conflict had provided any number of mutually hostile explanations. The third, if a two-hundred-and-ninety-two-year cycle had been reliable, would have impressively commemorated Europe's year of revolutions in 1848. The popularisers of science, however, were pointing out that "by the Newtonian theory of gravitation the period would have been delayed by such planets as the comet nearly approached." And among them the Frenchman Arago was able, though his eyesight had failed in 1850, to guess at a return at some point between 1856 and 1860. The appointment for June, 1857, and the calculations of a collision-course, were offered from less regarded sources. But to those who scrutinised the railway-bookstalls of the brothers W. H. Smith for signs of the public appetite it was evident that anything by Dr Cumming "goes down amazingly."

Another established reputation, that of *Old Moore's Almanac*, was not to be risked on an apocalypse. "The rising of the sun and the going down of the same," Old Moore reassured his readers, "are true to their appointed times." Those who wanted more for their penny could turn the pages to find that "India will be in an excited state, and great judgement is required to preserve order." As to order at home, the followers of Zadkiel, *alias* Tao Sze, *alias* Samuel Smith of Brompton Road, might expect by about February a change in the administration, with Palmerston "hard pushed to hold his place as Premier." But for confidence in the essential structure of society there was nobody like Old Moore: "There will be many worshippers at the shrine of Hymen, to secure that best of earthly blessings which is domestic bliss."

II

JANUARY
How They Met Themselves

IN THE LAST days of 1856 a large seal undertook a venturesome journey up the River Thames. Since it passed unperceived, or at least unrecognised, the serpentine reaches of its progress to the Pool of London call for no particular description: except to draw attention to a portent for 1857 in the overweening shadow of the Big Ship, building for the past two years at Millwall on the Isle of Dogs. For the iron-headed directors of the Eastern Steam Navigation Company, Isambard Kingdom Brunel can dream at nearly thrice the length of the first gigantic *Great Western*. The shaft of the screw weighs sixty tons, and its four prodigious fans, as they lie upon the ground, remind the fanciful of the bladebones of some fossil monster of the pre-Adamite world. At the full width across her paddle-boxes it is estimated that the *Great Eastern* would just be able to steam, scraping the mansions on either side, up Portland Place: into which, say knowledgable longshoremen, pointing with their pipes at stem and stern of the rising construction, she is as likely to be launched as by any sideways nonsense into the Thames.

Sweet Thames, run softly. The right of Englishmen to die of cholera without the interference of meddlesome authority— a right exercised by some twenty thousand of them during a year monopolised by the Crimean War—had been curtly upheld by *The Times* when Edwin Chadwick retired from the Metropolitan Sanitation Board. But under Bazalgette the Great Sanitary Idea is gaining ground, and the river is gaining specific density, so that Dickens cannot cross London Bridge to entrain for Gad's Hill, and the long-desired house which is at last to be his, without wrinkling his sensitive nose.

Fishes that swim against the stream seemed to Ruskin to be pointing a moral law. But the grey seal's fortitude went unrecorded as it pushed forward between the barges and the wherries and the thrashing paddle-wheels; and under London Bridge, and under Southwark Bridge, the sleek pate breaking surface now and then among the drifting slats of Christmas orange-boxes, and the nondescript small carcases, and the liquid history's additive of semi-solid sewage; and so towards the next line of arches at Blackfriars.

From his rooms at Blackfriars, right at the corner of the old stone bridge, in a house sagging with decrepitude but projecting over the river the valuable feature of a three-sided window with a little balcony, Rossetti stared blankly out upon a prospect neither bright nor dark: "a white smutty day—piebald—wherein accordingly life seems neither worth keeping nor worth getting rid of. The thick sky has a thin red sun stuck in the middle of it . . . I am going to sleep."

Sleep. Sleepy uncertainty lapsing into worried slumber, waking into guilty lethargy, because the two halves of the dream would never fit. Not even if he were to marry the girl, as a couple of months earlier he had surprised himself by resolving to do. The impulse of decision had somehow been sidetracked, and Lizzie Siddal—frail stunner with the karate chop—had moved from languid decline to blasting fury, and left him for ever, so that after a few weeks she had to be fetched back from Bath. There was the web of another London winter, wispy with the river's miasma, to be spun about the somnambulants. But Spring Cottage, where Gabriel had now installed her, close to Keats's former home at the lower corner of Hampstead Heath, was considerably further from Blackfriars than her old lodgings in Weymouth Street. It made no difference whatever that it was quite near the house off Haverstock Hill in which Karl Marx, having somehow moved his family from the squalor of Soho, wrote so far into the night, and with ink so pale, that his eyes were painfully inflamed.

And the lonely seal swam on to shiver the dappled pinnacles below the new Houses of Parliament, and past the ancient horse-ferry, and the model prison on the corner of Millbank, from which convict-colonists were dispatched down-river towards the Antipodes with a Benthamite regard for the ultimate efficiency. Surely now we can imagine the patient creature beginning to regret the whole undertaking, the sludge on his whiskers, the running current, the sucking tide, and the burden of Ruskin's Pathetic Fallacy? But before the conceit can be well extended, the seal has been seen in Wandsworth Reach, and duly assassinated, and briefly commemorated in the public prints, and avenged in a roaring of North Sea tempest that wrecked forty vessels between Flamborough Head and Tynemouth and stranded upon Winterton beach in Norfolk a forty-eight-foot whale. All of which was a far and indeed inaudible cry from Blackfriars and the wombat-slumbers, obtuse and furry, of Dante Gabriel Rossetti.

Fresh and pat to her brother's predicament came Christina's Christmas Eve sonnet:

> One face looks out from all his canvases . . .

Not a remarkable discovery, perhaps, nor one that required Miss Rossetti to *like* Miss Siddal. The empathy commemorated in the *Oxford English Dictionary*, where it is Christina who supplies the definitive literary use of Gabriel's wombat, allowed her an anguished insight into the duality which had wrecked her own prospects of nuptial bliss and kept her brother dithering on the awful threshold. The ideal answer could be drawn but not achieved, impelling Gabriel in moods of depression such as this to work again at the drawing that he called *How they Met Themselves*, in which four fragments of personality, magically becoming two, propose the illusion of becoming one—like the companionable Brownings, perhaps; those two small people who, in the autumn of Gabriel's recent crisis, had followed the swallows southwards again, making for the Italy of his ancestors, "taking meanwhile so little room in any railway carriage, and hardly needing a double bed at the inn." As in the best contemporary fiction, the Brownings had been sped upon their way with a modest but sufficient legacy. Rossetti must make do with a sisterly sonnet, the primly affectionate epitaph upon nearly seven years of his wavering bondage to the Sid, the Number One Stunner, the child-woman-spirit ecstatically discovered behind a milliner's counter, imposed upon a whole circle as cult-image but at length reserved to one alone as lightly-breathing sitter and tormenting inspiration, Guggums and Goddess, Blessed Damozel and ranting bitch, playmate and Pillar of Salt:

> Not as she is, but was when hope shone bright,
> Not as she is, but as she fills his dream.

Lest the dream degenerate, the model must be creative in her own right, the love-object become agent, her competitive talents win from kind-hearted Mr Ruskin a subsidy of genius, though indeed so delicately offered as almost to turn her back again into object: "If you would be so good as to consider yourself as a piece of wood or Gothic for a few months, I should be grateful to you." But what could save the dream's unearthly element from the creeping triumph of sensuality, a triumph which Gabriel could and did celebrate elsewhere, concurrently and without evident scruple?

There was but one remedy, the period remedy known as consumption. Riverside vapours, Bohemian habits, pharmaceutical vagaries played their part, but surely as abettors of an inward necessity for the sword to wear out its sheath, the desirable flesh to become translucent, and Lizzie to make what she could of the neurotic privilege. "Nobody is interested in my soul," she once complained. This was not strictly true. But by 1857 the devaluation of a corporeal presence that had once been a passionately realised asset had gone dangerously far. Memories and impulses only partly understood might still bring Rossetti to the committal into which he could be neither frozen nor shouted. But to dice with death for a lustreless treasure was not really in his line.

It is a relationship of more enduring interest than all the multiple fornications of The Other Victorians. And in this year in which anything could happen one detects a reversion of the visual imagination to a particular conjunction of figures. Whether it is *The Wedding of St George* or some other trendy filling for a square frame, ideal love affects a sedentary consummation. Just so, as dusk invaded the room above the river, so quietly that the double click of the lamplighter's pole in Chatham Place was a distinct and familiar signal, Gabriel and his Guggums must so often have disposed themselves. But once in special, when we can fancy— following the scent through a lifetime of Rossetti's almost unread verse—that she welcomed him returning to his pad

> And sat down at my feet upon the floor
> Leaning against my side. But when I felt
> Her sweet head reach from that low seat of hers
> So high as to be laid upon my heart,
> I turned and looked upon my darling there,

And marked for the first time how tall she was . . .
　　　She gazed at me with eyes
As of the sky and sea on a grey day,
And drew her long hands through her hair, and asked me
If she were not a woman; and then laughed:
And as she stooped in laughing, I could see
Beneath the growing throat the breasts half-globed
Like folded lilies deepest in the stream.

In Titian's *Sacred and Profane Love* connoisseurs have established the sacred figure as the one *without* her clothes, a tenderly voluptuous Celestial Venus confronting the draped and demure model of Profane or Natural Attachment. Probing behind the etiolated academic conventions the Pre-Raphaelites had emerged, not with the realism of Etty's naked housemaids but with such a glowing wardrobe of properties that the semi-divine Lizzie had been condemned to remain fully clothed even in her bath, the while Millais painted the drowned Ophelia and the water chilled as the candles beneath the tub guttered one by one. But the old hobgoblins were not exorcised. They peopled the dreams which in 1857 were being regularly reported and discussed in the new *Psychological Journal*. And the dream-world itself could be either a metaphor for all that could aspire beyond the grossness of daily appetite, or else a hellish repository into which one must at all costs avoid being sucked.

It was something of the latter sort for Florence Nightingale. Solitary vice, as Rossetti told Ford Madox Brown in the matter of the Ruskin scandal, takes many forms, and Miss Nightingale's Inferno was the Kingdom of Dreams. By the end of 1843 she had identified her besetting sin, and the turn of each year, bringing the social round from one great house to another, which she hated scarcely less than she hated herself for not hating it enough, brought also the annual report to her other self. The season's saturnalia, the organisation of food and drink and clothes and transport, the house-parties of up to eighty sleeping-guests, had been such a background as Hieronymus Bosch might have painted for a mystical escape, not out of the world of reality but into it. On the eve of 1845, prostrated and protected by psychosomatic collapse, Florence had been alone in the big yellow house at Embley in Hampshire, her parents and sister at Waverley for the ball, her new pink dress with black lace flounces still in its box, a little black teapot on the hob in her room, lamplit papers on her knee, the window-curtains parted on a world of hard frost and bright moonlight, three hares gambolling on the lawn, all else dead: but the deadly pride of life still unsubdued in Florence Nightingale. At the next year's end, after a shocked parental ban on the notoriously immoral calling of hospital-nursing: "I shall never do anything and am worse than dust and nothing." But the winter of 1847–8 had wrapped her in the enchantments of Rome, the adopted beggar-girl, the convent-visits, the first subversion of the wealth-burdened Sidney Herbert, so that this time "the happiest New Year I have ever spent" could be guiltlessly danced in.

Not every tortured soul could so prolong and vary the Via Dolorosa. Egypt in 1849 with the generous Bracebridges, returning by way of Greece, where the furies could be confronted in the Cave of the Eumenides itself; Corfu and Trieste, where the enemy for once let her go, but came again with "long days of absolute slavery" until "I lay in bed and called on God to save me." Which for a while He did, moving in ways made less mysterious of late by Mr Thomas Cook: so that the distracted virgin, travelling with two tortoises, a baby owl called Athena, a cicada called Plato, a personal maid called Trout and a quantity of luggage, was enabled to make her longed-for call at the Kaiserswerth Retreat in Germany. And still the turn of 1850–1, the first New Year's Eve of Tennyson's carillon, could neither ring out the false nor in the true. Despair laid hold of her:

> My present life is suicide. Slowly I have opened my eyes to the fact from the habit of dreaming which, like gin-drinking, is eating out my vital strength.

For "like" read "as if it were," and ponder once again upon the deep and inward necessity of the Crimean War, which afforded Richard Burton some opportunity for recovering his spirits, and set the Rev. Charles Kingsley capering uncontrollably with the itch to be at Inkerman, and opened for Florence Night-ingale, at last, the road through Scutari.

The New Year milestones of reflection and resolution glim-mered diminishingly behind her. By the Christmas of 1856 the chief significance of Embley was that it lay close to Broadlands, the pillared country mansion of Lord Palmerston, whom she was thus able to distract from his shooting and his billiards for long enough to capture his support for her current onslaught on the official plans for Netley Military Hospital. Melting back into London and her paper-jungle for the broader campaign against War Secretary Lord Panmure, she took with her certain domestic annoyances of a serio-comic intensity which were still not to be shaken off. As she wrote to her father on 12 January:

> In a difficult life (and mine has been more difficult than most) it is always better clearly to decide for oneself
>> what grievances one will bear, being unavoidable,
>> what grievances one will escape from,
>> what grievances one will try to remove.

It was seldom so clear-cut as that ("I *must* remember," she told herself severely, "not to treat God as my private secretary"). But it was sensible to have left Embley before Mr and Mrs Monckton Milnes arrived for their New Year call, for Richard Monckton Milnes had once been her olive-blond messenger from the Kingdom of Dreams. She had even rejected another suitor while she considered his offer of marriage, but five years of such skirmishing were enough for Richard, who then delivered an ultimatum. Controlling her anguish, Florence turned him down, whereafter he married the pleasant and eligible Annabel Crewe.

It was evidently by the grace of God that this philanthropic dillettante had failed in his desultory siege of Florence Nightingale. Member of Parliament, heir to the Fryston estate in Yorkshire and "an artist in social astonishments," his mild but amiable talents were chiefly spent in the cultivation of a wide panorama of friendships. His unassuming attention to good works on behalf of young delinquents was matched by his conspiratorial zest in assembling one of the finest of pornographic libraries. Of the second of these hobbies Florence presumably knew nothing, but she could not fail to be stirred by the first. "He had the same voice and manner," she mused long afterwards, "for a dirty brat as for a duchess." Carlyle said that Monckton Milnes would have made an excellent President for a Society for the Amalgamation of Heaven and Hell. But he did not really reconcile the tiresome dualities. He simply ignored them.

In political affairs the scepticism of a man like Monckton Milnes seemed at this moment to be strangely pervasive. The alliance of Radical pacifism with big business had begun to look hollow, but even the factions of the Right had misgivings about wars undertaken without the formality of summoning Parliament, such as the two exercises offered for 1857. The first of these was an intervention in Persia, arising out of a mishandled personal squabble between "that ass Murray," as Foreign Secretary Lord Clarendon called his man on the spot, and an irascible Shah. The second was a more distant, and thus more expensive, embroilment with the Chinese authorities in Canton. In this case the man on the spot, Sir John Bowring, happened to be a member of the Peace Society and a political associate of Bright and Cobden. A reputation for commercial and linguistic expertise had projected him from the ranks of the opposition to the post of plenipotentiary at Hong Kong, where he had now distinguished himself by arranging for a naval bombardment of the Canton business quarter on the doubtful pretext that a vessel against which the Chinese had taken action for piracy was alleged to have been flying the British flag. When Bowring's despatches reached London, the Government hastily approved his measures. But the *Saturday Review*, when the thing began to be talked about, laid its editorial finger on a difficulty:

It used to be easy—nay, indeed, it was esteemed a national duty— to hate a Frenchman, and, more recently, it may have been easy to hate a Russian. The Afghans at one time enjoyed a fine share of the detestation of Englishmen; but it never was easy, at any time, to hate a Chinaman.

The defect was not beyond remedy. But at a time of vocal pressure for a reduction in military expenditure and the income-tax, the emotional effort was perhaps too much to expect.

Railing at the ill, in a domestic sense, seemed more in season than fighting for the good. A year of external peace had been, in Greville's estimate, "stained beyond all precedent with frightful crimes of every sort and kind, horrible murders, enormous frauds, and scandalous robberies and defalcations." The first month of 1857 provided the revelations of forgery and fraud for which Leopold Redpath and William James Robson were both sentenced to transportation. But this convenient penalty had been almost abandoned in face of increasingly strong objections from the receiving end. Within the realm the legislation and the accommodation for penal servitude were alike inadequate, and the "ticket-of-leave" system was a vexatious expedient.

Nothing is so sombre that the valiant cannot meet it with a smile, and while *Punch* made merry with the danger from garotters in the unlighted suburbs, the theatre flourished with farces exploiting the droll endeavours of city merchants to defend their homes against a wave of breaking and entering. Security of property, it was seriously agreed, was not what it had been in 1851, when the catalogue of the Great Exhibition had cited it, along with freedom of commerce, as a prime foundation of the national greatness. As for security of life, the deterrent and educative properties of public execution were now under open challenge.

Homicide itself was caught in the flux of values. Thomas Wainewright, the poisoner of Jacobean stature flaring with the Romantic sunset, had reached a quiet extinction in Tasmania, a transported felon with no companion but his cat and no consolation but the consciousness of living, killing, robbing and dying like an artist and a gentleman. The fact of a man's being a poisoner, as Oscar Wilde would come to insist, is nothing against his prose. But the prose of William Palmer's life-story, rushed out for a sale of twenty-five thousand copies on the railway-bookstalls, was none of his making. He even cheated the ten thousand *afficionados* who invaded his Staffordshire township of Rugely for his execution, giving them no word of a speech from the scaffold. The hangman had done reasonably well for himself by making a rope at twice the length required and selling it in six-inch souvenirs. But a sober section of Rugely's inhabitants, not relishing the publicity, sent a deputation to London to plead for a change in the town's name. Only on their way home did they realise that Lord Palmerston's affably suggested solution—that the place should be re-named after himself—would not do at all.

Palmer the Poisoner, after all, just *may* not have been guilty of the particular crime that hanged him. On the Lord Chief Justice of England, however, the trial had left a certain mark. To put it shortly, Lord Campbell had a thing about poisons. For this steadily successful Lowland Scot it had been a matter of professional diligence to pierce, in a two-day summing-up, a labyrinth of curious and conflicting medical testimony. But even an applauded verdict left untouched the general, subtle and corrosive evil, supported as it was by the availability of poisons and the laws of evidence.

In Campbell's own native land, but beyond his jurisdiction and outside his present considerable knowledge, Miss Madeleine Smith of Glasgow had recently become aware that her lover, Pierre l'Angelier, was earning no more than £50 a year. Another suitor worth £400, appearing at the crucial moment and with the support of her parents, was accepted. But the recovery of passionately compromising letters presented difficulties, and at the end of January Miss Smith first sent out for prussic acid. At about the same time a Chinese baker at Hong Kong so far forgot himself as to mix arsenic in his flour. The destruction of Chinese life and property in the bombardment of Canton had been warmly resented; Sir John Bowring and his family, as well as other British households, were on the baker's delivery round; and the man had been paid enough to discharge the debts that weighed upon him and make a bolt for Macao.

The fact of a man's being Lord Chief Justice is nothing against his prose. Lord Campbell had begun his career as a journalist, and something more than the Dickens gin-punch had moistened his lips, something more than the Dickens *bonhomie* had flushed his cheeks, on the evening when he raised his glass to declare that he would have given all his legal honours and achievements to have written *Pickwick*. What he had himself completed over the past twelve years was his *Lives of the Lord Chancellors* in twelve volumes, relieving the task at intervals with the *Lives of the Chief Justices*. Considering their bulk, the books commanded a gratifying circulation, and here already was a fourth printing of the *Chancellors*. But here also were the January reviews, lamenting (as a not untypical instance) that so lofty a luminary seemed "never to have thought of applying his practised sagacity to the investigation of historical truth." The most that was conceded by the stricter sort of critic was that Lord Campbell's intellect, "though coarse, is undoubtedly robust and athletic." But then superior comments of this kind were even cast in the direction of Charles Dickens, who not only prospered exceedingly but was once again drawing to his New Year entertainment an invited audience of high social tone. In the theatre converted to professional standards from the schoolroom of the Dickens children in Tavistock House, upwards of ninety guests could be seated—with due but not excessive allowance for crinolines—on each of the four January nights allotted to the performance. And Lord Campbell was the most distinguished of half a dozen law-lords who ignored the novelist's treatment of their calling in the pleasure of his invitation.

Only one guest—Angela Burdett-Coutts—needed persuasion, and she needed a great deal of it to get her down from Highgate. The relations of this characterful heiress with the writer who aided and abetted her good works was important enough, in its strange mixture of reserve and intimacy, to provide a challenge on this single point: the lady's rooted disapproval of the histrionic impulse which was to become for her admired friend (as perhaps she divined) a finally suicidal obsession. "Must do it—can't help it," he had told her during his December preparations. "I really cannot bear that it should pass over without your seeing it." Although the play had been written by Wilkie Collins, whose somewhat disreputable character might have come to Miss Coutts's ears, Dickens was "quite sure that its whole influence is softening and good." And it might well be the last time that Clarkson Stanfield would paint the scenery, for that well-loved Royal Academician was getting infirm and ill. A few days later Dickens tried again: "I could not quite give you up without a struggle." And on 2 January:

> I should very much like you only to see a Sunset—far better than anything that has ever been done at the Diorama or any such place. There is a Rehearsal tonight (no one here but the company), and this Sunset, which begins the play, will be visible at a quarter before 8; lasting ten minutes. If you come, you need speak to nobody but Georgina and me—and nobody need so much as see you to recognise you. But I don't press you, and don't look for an answer.

What he did not tell her was that, in the intervals of writing *Little Dorrit*, getting out *Household Words* and choosing overall-material for the inmates of the Home for Fallen Women, he had been taking twenty-mile walks to learn and rehearse, in full voice, his lead in the melodrama, "to the great terror of Finchley, Neasden, Willesden and the adjacent country." And in the end he got her to Tavistock House, to witness the phenomenal sunset and stay for the agonies and ecstasies of *The Frozen Deep*.

The Arctic setting of the play's second act had been inspired by public concern with the fate of Sir John Franklin and his men in their quest for the North-West Passage:

To that white region where the lost lie low,
Wrapp'd in their mantles of eternal snow;
Unvisited by change, nothing to mock
Those statues sculptured in the icy rock,
We pray your company . . .

Thus the Prologue, spoken behind the curtain by John Forster, gloomily aware that Collins had supplanted him in the valuable confidence of Dickens. Except for Lady Franklin, who was even then lobbying for a new search-attempt where so many had drawn blank, the event had at last established itself. But the guarded secret of *The Frozen Deep* was in a dénouement that looked forward in style to Sidney Carton's "far, far better thing," and the applause of endless audiences for *The Only Way*. Dying as Richard Wardour under the Union Jack, with a last blessing upon the girl of his heart and the rival to whom his sacrifice has united her, Dickens on those four January nights did more than suspend disbelief. Alike at the session graced by the Duke of Devonshire and at that reserved for the household staff and local tradesmen, the sobs were unrestrained, the bravos vociferous, the intermission only just long enough to repair tear-stained cheeks and cramped intestines for the side-splitting farce which completed the entertainment.

It was a high point of the season, and something which Mr Thackeray, deprived by his wife's mental illness of a mother for his girls and a hostess for his home, could not have attempted to match. As a regular guest at the Tavistock House theatricals, he had been known to roll right off his chair with mirth during one of the comic pieces. But his offer to sing a song between the acts of a charity matinee of the Dickens promotion had been declined, like the application for the vacancy of Dickens's illustrator which had long ago brought the two men face to face for the first time. In the decade since *Vanity Fair* the conveyor-belt of serialised fiction had run well for both of them; and if the instalment of *Dombey and Son* that carried the death of Paul Dombey to sixty thousand stricken households had almost floored Thackeray ("There's no writing against this—it's stupendous") there was some reassurance in *Little Dorrit* ("stupid stuff"). The demoniacal energy of Dickens as a barnstormer was beyond the reach or taste of Thackeray, whose large physique concealed a delicate constitution, while his profits from the platform—a new form of literary dividend—were offset by a tendency to become horribly bored by his own lectures. Stiffly dressed, spectacles on nose, he would clutch the reading-desk, not waving but drowning. A candid friend told him what he needed was a piano.

He didn't need a piano. Now that *The Four Georges* lectures were to be given in London, the snorts of disapproval over the success of his American tour—exposing the frailties of British sovereigns to a tribe of rude Republicans—were just what his management needed to pack them in at five shillings a seat, and to compensate the lecturer's personal tedium at the rate of a guinea a minute.

Dr Livingstone was cheaper at the Mansion House on the spiritual and commercial prospects of savage Africa, and the ill-paid Richard Owen had a lecturer's monopoly in fossil mammalia and reptilia. The cream of the winter's intellectual spread was to be found at the Royal Institution, where Michael Faraday's exciting scientific expositions so often robbed the Queen of her husband's evening company and raised in other minds disturbing possibilities. One of his lectures for the new season, "the result of long thinking, and curiously perplexing to the audience," was reported by Arthur Hugh (*Amours de Voyage*) Clough to Emerson in America:

> It was on Conservation of Forces—no force is ever lost or lessened— it is only transferred . . . How does this apply to Gravitation? . . . If the planets were removed, would the sun in respect of gravitation be inoperative? . . . Double the number of planets, will the amount of gravitating power in the sun be doubled? This, he says, has always been an utter perplexity to him.

With Cumming predicting the cataclysm and Faraday confessing his perplexity, it might be simpler to take the children to the Royal Polytechnic, where the programme included demonstration-lectures on optical illusions, a miniature model theatre, conjuring-tricks and comical contrivances, an entirely new series of dissolving views and the gratuitous distribution, from a giant Christmas-tree, of "thousands of beautiful ornaments and Mappin's pocket-knives." All over town, ignoring the private challenge of the Tavistock House sunset, the competition of dioramas and panoramas was in full swing. The lead was still held by Albert Smith after thousands of performances at the Egyptian Hall of his illustrated Ascent of Mont Blanc and Tour of the Rhine. But

Title-page illustration from *The Keepsake* for 1857 edited by Miss Powers

Work. By Ford Madox Brown (detail). Carlyle and Maurice on right

Thackeray lecturing on *The Four Georges* in the Edinburgh Music-Hall, January, 1857

Professor Richard Owen lecturing on *Osteology and Palaeontology of the Mammalia* at the London Museum of Practical Geology, April, 1857

the Royal Colosseum, just east of Regent's Park, offered a confident and continuous festival of London by Day and Night, Mountain Torrents and Cascades, Pyrotechnic Displays and Music.

The pantomime at the Great National Standard Theatre relied for its obligatory transformation-scene on "the most beautiful, most costly, and complicated piece of machinery ever invented." At Astley's Royal Amphitheatre on the Surrey side, where Mr Cooke had done famously out of Shakespeare on horseback, the pantomime also was mainly equestrian. And at the Theatre Royal in the Haymarket *The School for Scandal* alternated with "juvenile nights" of *Babes in the Wood*, or *Harlequinade and the Cruel Uncle*, after which the portico began to shelter the nocturnal promenade of prostitutes. From the Princess's Theatre young Mr Dodgson, in London on his way back to Oxford, returned with prudent speed on the night of 21 January to the small Covent Garden hotel called the Old Hummums, after a thoroughly enjoyable double bill of *A Midsummer Night's Dream* and *Aladdin and the Wonderful Lamp*. The pantomime had been "beautifully got up, as everything at the Princess's is," and the *Dream* had a winsome Titania in Miss Kate Terry. Her little sister Ellen, who played Puck, was not yet of an age to ensnare the painter G. F. Watts. But she was just right for Lewis Carroll.

III

FEBRUARY

Sappho's Leap

THE COLD SPELL brought heavy snow over southern England and mortality in Regent's Park. In the first years of the Zoological Society's collection the lions, tigers, leopards and pumas had an average expectation of two years of life. Attributing this wastage to their close confinement in what were little better than dismounted menagerie-caravans, the management had rushed to the other extreme by constructing terraced dens, which exposed the tropical immigrants to the full rigours of winter and a rising share of the country's inflammatory diseases. These had now been appreciably countered by matting and artificial heat. But experiments in heating the badly ventilated monkey-houses produced barrowfuls of corpses on winter mornings until a new house was constructed, with an open stove. This was just across the path from the enclosure in which the wombat was happily reported to "bear the vicissitudes of the English climate without the necessity of any further protection than a wooden box well supplied with straw."

Like the young woman "of the costermonger class" described by Walter in one of the tireless encounters of *My Secret Life*, "they don't feel cold as we do." It was in the nature of Walter's interest to seek and enjoy the common physical factor, but to vary the basically invariable with a failed novelist's observation of social differences and the individual reactions of habit and character. But the ability to see the poor as a separate species, with Mayhew to break it down into sub-species and occupational mutations, was of immense value to middle-class philanthropy as to middle-class fiction.

The first of February fell on a Sunday, and at Harrow the prospect of snowballing marked the day white. Against that schoolboy pleasure there had to be set the often maddeningly extended chapel-sermons of Dr Vaughan, who on one occasion had brought a punch-drunk congregation rumbling to its feet with the

apparently dimittive words "And now to . . . ," only to thrust it
back as he continued: "And now to the principal theme for
today." In terms of a rapid expansion of numbers the school
had certainly prospered under Vaughan, who had been a prize
pupil of the late Dr Arnold and had only just missed succeeding
him as Headmaster at Rugby. In default of that nostalgic appointment he had devoted the past twelve years on Harrow Hill to
the declared ambition of "producing Christians and Gentlemen."
And Macaulay, if only for the sake of his nephew George Otto
Trevelyan, now in his last school year, felt glad that Dr Vaughan
was still in command. "After next October, the sooner he is
made a Bishop the better."

But this is not a year for smoothly virtuous courses. It is a
year for unthinkable influences, imprudent deviations, irreversible
impulses: such that a mitre for Vaughan, though indeed it waits
on offer a few years down the line, will mysteriously have to be
declined. Can we in the meantime reproach him for prohibiting
at Harrow the traditional use of feminine names for the younger
and prettier boys, and their assignment as "bitches" for the older
ones? Should we not rather admire the insidious power of a
classical curriculum that absorbed three-quarters of a public
school education, and the antique spell that could so direct
the lightnings of a beaten schoolboy's eyes as to pierce the black
serge carapace of Zeus himself? To end by seducing one's headmaster, as the boy Alfred Pretor had been formed to do, is not
given to every wrestler with the syntax of an epigram upon
Ganymede.

"All men go through an awful ordeal at school and college,"
wrote Charles Darwin's excellent wife, wondering about her own
boy and missing him. "It is only wonderful," she added, "what
good souls they turn out to be after all." It was wonderful too,
with what loyal fondness they were inclined to dwell, when they
reached an age and status for memoirs, on the healthy rigours of
their schooldays. Augustus Hare was on the whole exceptional
in recalling the blank uselessness of his Harrow education and the
ferocious bullying of small boys. Swinburne, who had been withdrawn from Eton for some time before he went to Oxford, did
not falter in his love for his school, but centred it on the pleasure
he had derived from exquisite and unforgettable floggings. At
a newer public school like Radley, where famished pupils had
been known to grub up the bulbs in the Headmaster's garden,

Charles Lutwidge Dodgson, walking over for a visit from Oxford in March, 1857, "was particularly struck by the healthy happy look of the boys and their gentlemanly appearance." What was most unusual, however, was the partitioning of the dormitories, "at a trifling expense in wood-work," so as to afford even the smaller boys a snug privacy that could be seen as "a kind of counterbalance to any bullying they may suffer during the day." If he could have been equally secure at Rugby from harassment at night, thought the sensitive Dodgson, "the hardships of the daily life would have been comparative trifles to bear." The inside and the outside view of school life are seldom identical, and the rage for official enquiry into the system was yet to come.

By the second Sunday of February the snow had gone from London in a wet and muggy thaw. At Harrow John Addington Symonds, now in his seventeenth year, put on his goloshes and went for a walk with his good clergyman friend Mr Smith, reciting Tennyson's *Oenone* to the bare and dripping trees. Herbert Spencer and T. H. Huxley took their usual Sunday stroll up the Finchley Road, in the general direction of Agnosticism. South of the river, in the Royal Surrey Gardens Music Hall, a small round man was exercising his mesmeric oratory, with the well-chosen text of "Cleanse Thou me from my secret faults," upon a mixed congregation of fully nine thousand persons. The Rev. Charles Spurgeon was not yet twenty-three, his clerical title had a limited acceptance, and his celebrated Tabernacle at Newington Butts was still to be erected. But his powerful command of voice and language, his impassioned assault upon trembling consciences, and his knack of homely illustrations, had made first his New Park Street Chapel in Southwark, and then the Exeter Hall off the Strand, too small for his growing Sunday following. And when he had first booked the great Surrey Gardens auditorium in the previous October, a mischievous call of "Fire!" at the height of his peroration had provoked a catastrophic panic from which, escaping in legendary circumstances, he extracted a wave of fresh publicity. Men of affairs and ladies of fashion were now to be seen among the crowds of common people for whom, had there been no deeper attraction, Spurgeon on the Awful Progress of Infidelity was a uniquely licensed Sabbath recreation.

Bored by the opening days of a Parliament returning after a recess extended to six months by four prorogations, Charles

Greville tried a Sunday afternoon of Spurgeon on this 8 February. He gave the preacher good marks for sincerity and fluency in the exposition of his text:

> He divided it into heads, the misery, the folly, the danger (and a fourth which I have forgotten) of secret sins, on all of which he was very eloquent and impressive. He preached for about three quarters of an hour, and, to judge of the handkerchiefs and the audible sobs, with great effect.

The slender, elegant figure of John Ruskin, in his long frock coat and his beautiful dark blue cravat, was also among the congregation. Just three years before, on 7 February, 1854, he had closed with his thirty-fifth birthday "what is at the highest average the first half of human life," and had begun to prepare for the sunset by counting with his diary-entries the number of days of life, work and sensation which he could still statistically expect. On this Sunday he made it 11,648: "Hear [sic] Mr Spurgeon on 'Cleanse thou me from secret faults'—very wonderful." Shortly afterwards he sent Spurgeon a hundred guineas for his building fund. Nor does anything forbid us to determine at this point in Ruskin's life the extirpation of "the evil that was its death," the conquest of his own secret fault which he would one day plead in desperate justification of a spotless love for Rose La Touche. The year's mysterious auguries are at work, and Spurgeon has not only earned Ruskin's subscription. More awkwardly for all concerned, he has converted Rose's father, the Anglo-Irish banker.

But to heal the ravages of a sense of sin was not within the preacher's mandate. The belief that the Victorians invented masturbation is plainly untenable. What the generation of Ruskin's fearsome nurse and his dominant parents had achieved, besides the patenting of a bloodcurdling range of contraptions for the preservation of purity, was a strategic concentration of guilt. The goat-foot god may have been hard to recognise in the creature that had been driven out into the desert to be painted by Holman Hunt. But the unidentified sin against the Holy Ghost was always, as it were, ready to hand. The inspiration of the Earl of Shaftesbury's lifelong labours for the poor and oppressed was his unshakeable Evangelical belief in "the total depravity of the human heart by nature." Nor could Gladstone win the crown of virtue without the agony of self-accusation ("Beast, fool, blackguard, puppy, reptile!"). Medical science itself, mounting its artillery of earthly punishments, found it easier to support the moralistic conspiracy than to follow a mere natural history lecturer like Huxley in his sceptical crusade— "the resolute facing of the world as it is when the garment of make-believe by which pious hands have hidden its uglier features is stripped off." Turning from the volumes of sermons in the early publishing lists for 1857 we may light upon Dr William Acton's authoritative *Functions and Disorders of the Reproductive Organs*, wherein the troubled enquirer can quickly ascertain:

> that the man will and must pay the penalty for the errors of the boy; that for one that escapes, ten will suffer; that an awful risk attends abnormal substitutes for sexual intercourse; and that self-indulgence long pursued, tends ultimately, if carried far enough, to early death or self-destruction.

It did not escape Dr Acton's observation that in the stages of mental disturbance which he attributed to such indulgence "religion forms a noted subject of conversation or delusion." But the climate in which he worked was enough to inhibit the inference that might have been drawn. It was enough also to persuade him that women were by nature what contemporary convention assumed them to be, the victims rather than the participants of man's sexuality. Though constrained to admit that cases of nymphomania were met with in lunatic asylums, he was prepared to say "that the majority of women (happily for them) are not very much troubled with sexual feeling of any kind." It was only to please her husband, he went on, that "a modest woman" would submit to attentions from which, "but for the desire of maternity, she would far rather be relieved."

As professional evidence in defence of the three-decker novel, this was formidable, and Acton himself had the satisfaction of going before many months were out into a second edition. But these were virtually the only references to women in his whole treatment of the reproductive topic. As though to atone for this neglect he produced in this same year another, and indeed a much better, book. But its unflattering subject was prostitution. In the end, perhaps, he would make his contribution to "the resolute facing of the world as it is." But his message for 1857 is that all indulgence hovers close to over-indulgence, which in any form that it may take, inside or outside of matrimony, is thoroughly dangerous; that careless spending of semen is as inevitably ruinous as careless spending of money; that even the life of dreams can be and must be controlled by a pure and resolute will; and that the wages of sin is death.

It is thus that the diligent doctor seems to join the mixed army of subversive warlocks and avenging angels, advancing for their different purposes upon a society that had allowed religious certainties to be shaken by doctrinal schism, and the saving secular arm to be palsied by creeping reform. "The age of spirit-rapping and of Mr Spurgeon," as the *Saturday Review* had perceived in a despondent moment, "the times in which Dr Cumming is an authority, and Joe Smith and Mr Prince are prophets—cannot cast stones at any 'dark ages'." Spurgeon had bounced back at once. "A true Christian," he told his mass-audience, " is one who fears God and is hated by the *Saturday Review*." Dr Cumming took longer to react, with an elaborate statement of his position which the offending journal eventually printed. Joseph Smith, whose disciples were establishing beside the Salt Lake in Utah a bourgeois Utopia with polygamy as an efficient stabiliser, had no reason to be aware of this particular stricture. And Mr Prince, who had his own Utopia in a two-hundred-acre Abode of Love near Spaxton in Somerset, was not noticeably disturbed. From upwards of a thousand devoted followers this former Anglican curate exercised the invidious privilege of selecting such ladies as were worthy of his prophetic embraces. And since the highest prize was that of public copulation after prayers, the chapel of Mr Prince's Agapemone was furnished with comfortable sofas. Another thoughtful touch was the provision of a billiard-table for those not directly involved, and the hourly expectation of the Last Trumpet must have given zest to the game.

The threat of the spirit-rappers, which the *Saturday Review* had placed first on the list, was clearly more insidious. "Spiritualistic experiments made by persons interested in the new electro-biological discoveries" were infiltrating both religion and science with a stream of double-agents. The most successful practitioner of the cult, Daniel Dunglas Home (a grandson of the tenth Earl), had for the time being transferred himself from his Sloane Street Academy to Paris, where he moved as "Mr Hume" in the highest circles. Earl Granville, President of the Council in Palmerston's Cabinet, crossed his tracks on one of his visits to the French capital:

> The evening ended in a lecture on table-turning, etc., in which the Emperor and Empress believe. A certain Mr Hume produces hands, raises heavy tables four feet from the ground with a finger, knocks on the Emperor's hand from a distance. The Emperor is rather pleased at the table coming more to him than to the others; but seeing Lady G. and me look incredulous, he broke off saying, "They think us mad, and Lord Granville will report that the alliance is on a most unstable footing."

The alliance was not entirely stable, but neither was English mahogany. In Bayswater and St John's Wood, in Battersea and Highgate, dining-tables skipped and tilted, objects of unexpected import materialised from beyond the shaded candle-light, and the voices of trance delivered their cryptic messages. Mesmerism had already had a long vogue. Monckton Milnes mesmerised a monkey. Florence Nightingale mesmerised her pet owl. Tennyson mesmerised Mrs Tennyson, and Harriet Martineau was regularly mesmerised for the relief of those lifelong infirmities which her dogged industry set at defiance. But Spiritualism was the new wave. In the aged but still active Robert Owen it might seem the last infirmity of a noble mind, a strange declension from the practical demonstration of soundly capitalised Socialism in the New Lanark industrial community. But younger people were taking to it as a serious and advanced pursuit.

North London had an active communications-centre in the pleasant retreat called the Hermitage, on Highgate West Hill, where Rossetti had been sharing the garden-studio in the days of his first passion for Lizzie Siddal as the "meek, unconscious dove"; and where Lizzie, after he had settled at Chatham Place, was taken to form her first new friendships in the circle of William and Mary Howitt, lapsed Quakers and ardent Spiritualists. Neither at the Hermitage nor in the séances of Home and others did Lizzie ever achieve convincing contact with the ghostly lover, "the great strong heart," to whom she scribbled wistful verses. Thin as a candle, pale as her own death-wish, she flickered from one table to another, sometimes alone, sometimes with Gabriel, who was not yet ready to torment himself with occult regrets. To help the atmosphere along, however, his rich voice would weave stories out of the strange experiences of people whom he knew: of the artist Watts, for instance, who "paints queer pictures of God and Creation," and was quite frequently favoured, while disclaiming any kind of psychic gift, with flashes of second sight and apparitions in the shrubbery; or of Tennyson, who could go off into a self-induced trance by the quiet repetition of his own name. On the night before the first intimation of his appointment as Poet Laureate, Tennyson had dreamed that Prince Albert was offering him the honour, and had awoken saying to himself, "So kind, so German!"

The Prince and the Queen had themselves experimented, one evening at Osborne in 1853, with a table which duly revolved. Victoria found the sensation peculiar, but while Albert lived she had no temptation to raise departed spirits. The best-rewarded sensibilities, perhaps, were those of Elizabeth Barrett Browning. In her demurely sovereign presence the agitation of the furniture could almost be counted upon. During her last return to London with Robert and their little boy, while she was finishing *Aurora Leigh*, a séance much talked of had sucked out of the darkness an airborne wreath, which had been seen to settle unerringly upon her small, ringletted head. Her husband's new volume, *Men and Women*, had a poor reception that year, but only the malicious attributed his hostility towards the Spiritualist cult to a sense of pique at the misdirection of the wreath. He held his fire for *Mr Sludge the Medium*, rejoicing meanwhile in the family success.

Success it certainly was. In nine books of blank verse, *Aurora Leigh* held its readers like the latest novel from Mudie's, and sent them reeling into 1857 with that "rush and glow and ardour of palpitating life" which for Swinburne, recalling the intoxication at a distance of forty years, would remain not only unforgettable but authentic. For Walter Savage Landor, almost ready to depart, the fire of life leaped suddenly with the generous passion of the verse. It smote Ruskin at the moment when he was adding to his firmly didactic *Elements of Drawing* an appendix setting down "in clear order, the names of the masters whom you may safely admire, and a few of the books which you may safely possess." This was intended in the first place for his students of the Working Men's College, but it could be trusted to carry much further. And here it comes: "Mrs Browning's *Aurora Leigh* is, as far as I know, the greatest poem which the century has produced in any language."

This pleasing verdict was facilitated by an *ex cathedra* reduction of the available competition in English: "Cast Coleridge at once aside, as sickly and useless; and Shelley, as shallow and verbose; Byron, until your taste is fully formed, and you are able to discern the magnificence from the wrong . . ." If Keats, whom Ruskin certainly admired, seems to be missing, and Blake also, it is because the rescue of both of them, under the pioneering influence of Monckton Milnes, had not yet reached the wider public. But in writing to Browning in Italy, Ruskin was prepared to dig deeper, finding in *Aurora Leigh* "the greatest *poem* in the English language, unsurpassed by anything but Shakespeare—*not* surpassed by Shakespeare's *sonnets*." He recovered himself in time to draw the authoress's attention to certain "sharp blemishes" in her work.

A critical minority agreed that there were blemishes—improprieties of theme and language, for instance, which it was startling to have to notice in a female writer. The Queen herself reached the indulgent decision that she liked *Aurora Leigh* "as I like poetry in all shapes." Within the royal circle, however, she let fall comments upon its "occasional coarseness."

> . . . Am I coarse?
> Well, love's coarse, nature's coarse—ah, there's
> the rub.

Thus Mrs Browning's baleful Lady Waldemar, who at a party appeared like this:

> She looked immortal. How they told,
> Those alabaster shoulders and bare breasts
> On which the pearls, drowned out of sight in milk,
> Were lost, excepting for the ruby-clasp!
> They split the amaranth velvet-bodice down
> To the waist or nearly, with the audacious press
> Of full-breathed beauty. If the heart within
> Were half as white?—but, if it were, perhaps
> The breast were closer covered and the sight
> Less aspectable by half, too.

This was deliberately advanced. Ruskin, too, was beginning to nibble at the problem that beauty and virtue do not necessarily, after all, walk hand-in-hand. But the pervasive modernism of *Aurora Leigh* was in the challenging self-projection of the authoress:

The world of books is still the world. I write.

There was all the difference between storming the masculine heights in this fashion, and tunnelling beneath them like Marian Evans under the guise of George Eliot. Not even the editor of *Blackwood's* had guessed that such felicitously observed *Scenes of Clerical Life* as he had just begun to publish in his January issue could have flowed from a woman's pen. Elizabeth Barrett Browning, on the other hand, had poured through the lips not only of Aurora but of every other character in the poem, male and female, the attributable comments of a prophetess.

One must move with the times. And this, as an elderly but anonymous observer could not but acknowledge, was 1857.

It is now thought clever for young ladies to be loud, positive and rapid; to come into a room like a whirlwind; to express ideas of their own in a language which, twenty years ago, would only have been understood in the stable.

In intellectual stables Mrs Browning's language could still give trouble. In an earlier work of hers, Ruskin had been beaten by "nympholeptic," which she had had to explain to him as "a word for a specific disease or mania among the ancients, that mystical passion for an invisible nymph common to a certain class of visionaries." In further enlightenment she shrewdly added that "we are all nympholepts in running after our ideals— none more so than yourself indeed." Now she had dropped "phalanstery" into her pentameters, and Ruskin objected that he had failed to find it in Dr Johnson's Dictionary.

It was musical, and it was an in-word, too recent a coinage to have been anticipated by Johnson, but irresistible for slotting into the key problem of Romney Leigh's philanthropic drive. The American philosopher Emerson, who admired the English trait of leaving government and power to gentlemen and "persons of superior tendency," had lately gone on record with the view that England was itself "a huge phalanstery, where all that man wants is provided within the precinct." But Emerson might be wrong. "We beseech thee, O Lord," a fellow-theologian had publicly prayed after one of his early lectures, "to deliver us from hearing any more such transcendental nonsense as we have just listened to." Romney Leigh's phalanstery in the poem was evidently the close descendant of Robert Owen's working model and the extravagant visions of Fourier, a planned complex of buildings to be occupied by a phalanx or commune, a miniature alternative society, a pilot-Utopia for the fugitives from the rat-race and the chain-gang. It had to be introduced in order to impress upon the young idealists of protest that systems would not cure what systems had produced. And the unfortunate Romney was made to lose his eyesight by an ungrateful act of arson before he could see it.

It is thus that life, the poem's incontrovertible life, brings the wealthy philanthropist into dependence upon the modern young woman who had declined to be dependent upon *him*. The feminism is explicit, but there is a reassuring wedding-bell to ring in its triumph. By getting her man *and* keeping her social conscience, Aurora refutes the Nightingale thesis that getting a man is not just an inadequate but a morally destructive female ambition. By bringing him to cry:

> The world waits
> For help. Beloved, let us love so well,
> Our work shall still be better for our love,
> And still our love be sweeter for our work

she decrees the scaling-down of the phalanstery, insidious in its suggestions of free love, wife-swapping and extra-parental child-rearing, to the emotional safety of the marital unit.

There was another admonition to be conveyed by *Aurora Leigh*: that marrying out of one's class is no way to raise the unfortunate. Insofar as there is any character except the voice of the poetess, the heroine is Marian Earle, the little sweated seamstress who, by running out on the wedding-day offered by her quixotic rescuer, contributed to the indelicacy of the work a nameless child and a chapter of underworld shame. The victory of her essential innocence and the nobility of her renunciation require for their establishment the stock theme of the Search for the Lost Lamb. This in turn demands from us a prior, if reluctant, glance at the Great Social Evil.

In the serious corners of *Punch*, no less than in the bulletins of rescue-societies, the recurrence of the awesome phrase gives 1857 the colour of a campaign-year, and an evidently propitious one for the printing of Dr Acton's *Prostitution Considered in Its Moral, Social and Sanitary Aspects in London & Other Large Cities and Garrison Towns*. Even *Household Words*, from which Dickens normally excluded such things, became excited at this point by the nightly scene at the junction of Piccadilly and Regent Street, before anybody had the occasion or the idea to commemorate the puritan Earl of Shaftesbury by a statue of Eros:

> It is always an offensive place to pass, even in the daytime; but at night it is absolutely hideous, with its sparring snobs and flashing satins, and sporting gents and painted cheeks, and brandy-sparkling eyes, and bad tobacco and hoarse horse-laughs and loud indecency.

But since the writer of the article was the family-entertainer Albert Smith, some allowance must be made for professional rivalry.

Close to this central point were the Argyll Rooms in Windmill Street—not a brothel but a recognised place for a pick-up, where Walter of *My Secret Life* initiated some of his essays in practical sexology. In 1857 the resort was actually closed down by the Metropolitan Magistrates. But their interference drew protests from "several hundred of the nobility." The Argyll was soon back in business, and the active seraglios and houses of assignation—Kate Hamilton's, the Archery Rooms, the cigar-divans and so on—ran no risk so long as disturbances and breaches of the peace were avoided. The gaieties of Cremorne and other survivors from the tea-gardens of the eighteenth century had only to be supervised, according to Dr Acton, by a policeman "in an amiably discreet position where his presence could in no way appear symptomatic of pressure."

On the one hand are the archives, both grave and gay, of top-level debauchery: on the other the perseverance of Walter and the more chastely recorded investigations of Mayhew, who in *London Labour and the London Poor* arrived at a catalogue of six classes of prostitutes and several sub-castes. And the evidence points to 1857 as the historic moment of emergence from the underworld for the craft's most glittering aristocrats. Among those marked for the highest distinction as seeded players was the twenty-year-old daughter of a struggling Plymouth musician, who would have had to struggle less if he had not sold the rights of his composition *Kathleen Mavourneen* for a few pounds in a tight corner. With the adopted name of Cora Pearl the girl was now the current favourite of the proprietor of the Argyll Rooms, and precisely poised for the invasion of Paris, the conquest of primacy among the *grandes horizontales* and the final immortality in her own land of an entry in the *Dictionary of National Biography*. Freed from Cora's competition on the home ground, Laura Bell could still hold court in Grosvenor Square, though she had now become outwardly respectable as Mrs Thistlethwaite and was suspected of religious leanings. Celebrity of a kind was indeed to be hers, but the special service which she had given to England was somehow overlooked when honours were distributed. In 1850, the year of her London début at the age of twenty-one (she had served her apprenticeship in Dublin), Laura had achieved the conquest of Jung Bahadur, Nepal's Chief Minister, Kingmaker and Man of Destiny, on his English visit. In 1857 this chambering and wantonness was to find (as many thought) its romantically Oriental sequel when Jung Bahadur and his Gurkhas, in the burning light of crisis, rendered to Queen Victoria (or more correctly to the East India Company) the recompense earned by Laura Bell.

With such horizons in view one can accept Mr Gladstone's testimony that "these women dread, yes, actually dread going back into the kind of ordered, decent world they have left behind." But although Gladstone's undergraduate forays for reclamation had got him into trouble with the Oxford Proctors he could now, at forty-six, show at least a few successes in his nightly quarterings, from Park Lane eastwards to Ludgate Hill, of the capital's raffish centre. For the scale of the problem, the highest of a wide range of estimates—a figure of eighty thousand as the metropolitan population of prostitutes—can be found (secreted in a metaphor) in *Aurora Leigh*. The contribution of the *Lancet* in 1857 was the bland statement that one London dwelling in sixty was a brothel and one female in sixteen a whore. Dr Acton's calculations, which are not necessarily more reliable than anyone else's, suggested a reduction over the previous decade. The moral crusade had at any rate made sufficient ground with its Anglican, Catholic and non-denominational refuge-centres for the trade to take notice and organise its own defence. It was an advantage, of course, to be so sited that legislators could be conveniently lobbied after the cry of "Who goes home?" And the resourceful Mrs Jeffries, with her strategically placed chain of Westminster houses of pleasure, was able for nearly thirty years to impede the fixing of a legal age of consent. It was in this sombre context that Old Glad-Eye, as the prowlers of the better districts called the well-known gentleman with the stout walking-stick, would respond to their advances by courteously raising his hat and inviting them to come home for a nice talk and the hot meal with which his wife would welcome them. A liking for women, such as Gladstone retained all his life, is not the worst of reasons for saving them. His challenge to scandal was fearless and continuous, but we have to await the further volumes of his complete diaries to identify what their scrupulous editor has called "one particular friendship with a courtesan who exchanged physical for spiritual influence."

The connection of Charles Dickens with the moral campaign was rather different. He made himself indispensable to Angela Burdett-Coutts in the management of her establishment for reclaiming the fallen at Shepherd's Bush, which she insisted on calling Urania Cottage. There were polite battles to be fought with her from time to time over what Dickens considered her excessive and indeed vengeful righteousness. But just now it was the drains that were on his mind, the parlour having suddenly proved uninhabitable and the whole house fast becoming so. Assuring Miss Coutts that "the drainage is distinctly our business," and would be thirty or forty pounds well spent, he took the opportunity of adding: "The gas is now at the gate. Would you like it taken into the house?"

Dickens was a great fixer of such things. He was also a great roamer of the London night. But the pamphlet for the cause which he had composed some years earlier had been left to Gladstone and others to distribute. It began:

You will see, on beginning to read this letter, that it is not addressed to you by name. But I address it to a woman—a very young woman still—who was born to be happy, and has lived miserably; who has no prospect before her but sorrow, or behind her but a wasted youth; who, if she has ever been a mother, has felt shame instead of pride in her own unhappy child.

You are such a person, or this letter would not be put into your hands . . .

A promising opening, but not for the purposes of respectable fiction. In that department the nearest approach to the Great Social Evil that Dickens had allowed himself was in the search, in *David Copperfield*, for a named and loved and lost Little Em'ly ("who *must* fall," he confided to a friend, "there is no hope for her") in the terrible urban maw that demanded its perpetual tribute of rural innocence. But in the climate of Pre-Raphaelite "realism" (which Dickens had savagely attacked on its first appearance) the visual possibilities of the theme received serious attention. Holman Hunt, who had finished *The Awakening Conscience* on the day before his departure for the Holy Land, leaving it to acquire fame and a sale during his absence, was now obligingly repainting the girl's face for the picture's purchaser, who had found its strained eloquence too much for his own and his friends' composure. Rossetti, complaining that Hunt had infringed the copyright of his idea, was still tinkering, after several years, with what he called his "town subject."

It is here that the Social Evil becomes tangled with problems incidental to the artist's calling, the recovery of lost sheep with the search for models, the capture of the rarer stunners with the question of their domestication. The model who posed for *The Awakening Conscience*—in a rather tiring position, as half-arisen from the lap of venery—had all that the part required: or rather, everything except the possibility of being recalled to homely purity, in the manner of the picture, by the pianoforte score of *Oft in the Stilly Night*. Yet Annie Miller had so wrought upon Hunt's confused sensibilities that he had arranged to have her educated with a view to matrimony.

It was an imprudent project, but not entirely unusual. Ford Madox Brown, several years older than his friends, had quietly selected (after the early death of his first wife) a fifteen-year-old village girl, and had trained her through years of obscure indigence until she could be acknowledged as the Angel in the House. Augustus Egg of the Royal Academy had a wife to whom nobody could be introduced. To find anything like Elizabeth Siddal in a shop off Leicester Square was clearly considered exceptional, and it was still hard to be sure whether she was or was not engaged to Rossetti. But Annie Miller, whom Hunt had acquired at about the same time as the discovery of Lizzie, was something else again. She had none of that air of having come down in the world, that hint at an ancestral escutcheon,

THE GREAT SOCIAL EVIL. Time:—Midnight. A Sketch not a Hundred Miles from the Haymarket. *Bella.* "AH! FANNY! HOW LONG HAVE YOU BEEN GAY?"

Drawn for *Punch*, 1857, by John Leech, who is said to have had it published in the absence, and against the better judgment, of the editor, Mark Lemon

The 1857 Elections. By "Phiz"

Chatterton. By Henry Wallis

The Wedding of St George and Princess Sabra. By D. G. Rossetti

that hung intriguingly about Miss Siddal. Liveliness and physical beauty alone had enabled Annie to advance from an illiterate childhood in the squalor of Cross Keys Yard, and though Hunt's attentions may have stirred in her the ambition of material self-improvement, his proprietary assumption of a reforming mission made no appeal. He had not been long out of England before the seventh Lord Ranelagh had become all that might be said to go with the drinking of champagne from Annie Miller's slipper.

This grand liaison, as it happened, was more easily concealed from Hunt on his return than the extension of Annie's services as a model beyond the short list of reliable artist-friends which he had drawn up before departing. The roster had not included the name of Rossetti, but Gabriel had ways of getting over that. Lizzie had at this juncture been packed off to France for a few months at Ruskin's expense. Annie had a comparable abundance of red-gold hair, and a contrasting supply of flesh, complaisance and gaiety. She enjoyed going out to the alfresco pleasures of Cremorne, or preparing cozy suppers of roast mutton and gooseberry tart to sustain the indoor pleasures of Gabriel's company, or drawing all eyes at a private view as the model for *The Awakening Conscience*, or visiting the Zoo to make faces at the wombat. Rossetti, as if he needed a pretext, made some more sketches for his "town subject"—an honest rural type reclaiming errant daughter from urban degradation, the title to be *Found*. "Hunt stole my idea," he remarked in his nonchalant way, "so I stole his model."

He might even have got away with it as far as Hunt was concerned, for the complex and often strained relationship of the two artists had something enduring about it. But someone was bound to tell Lizzie, and Lizzie would have plenty to say. So, in different language, would Christina—if we accept that her long poem on the compulsory topic of spiritual *versus* sensual passion (*Look on this Picture and on this*) reflected her brother's ambivalence; and that it is Annie Miller who here emerges from her lessons in elocution and deportment in a character to set beside Mrs Browning's Lady Waldemar:

> You, my saint, lead up to heaven, she lures down to sin . . .
> She's so redundant, stately:— in truth now have you seen
> Ever anywhere such beauty, such a stature, such a mien?
> She may be queen of devils, but she's every inch a queen.

D

Holman Hunt's intentions in 1857, though a torment to himself and a bewilderment to his friends, were still honourable, and he continued to pay for Annie's education. But he had moved from Chelsea to the patrician environment of Campden Hill, and beyond her modelling visits to his studio she was free as a bird.

Suddenly, something in the February air brought to the brink of decision the intermittent but always unsatisfied yearnings of artists for their own sort of phalanstery, for some experiment in communal living which might revive the spirit of the defunct Pre-Raphaelite Brotherhood. It was the younger men, William Morris and Edward Burne-Jones, who had resolved on the quay-side at Le Havre, at the end of their undergraduate tour in France, that art rather than religion ought to inspire a new monastic ideal. But it was Rossetti, basking in the warmth of their admiration, who was now most taken with the idea of a joint establishment, and celibacy was no longer to be a qualification. The Browns, Ford Madox and Emma, were now living in Kentish Town, with Lucy, the child of the earlier marriage, and a new infant Arthur: they must be brought into the project as a family. Lizzie sounded agreeable (Gabriel's "wishes as to the scheme would entirely depend on hers"), and Burne-Jones must bring his affianced Georgiana. Possible properties were inspected, the disposal of bedrooms gravely considered. Only Morris, among the candidates for communal living, was so far completely unattached: and he, with a useful private income of £900 a year, had shown promise by purchasing the glowing image of *April Love*, by Arthur Hughes, from its poor placing on the walls of the Academy, where Ruskin had singled it out: "Exquisite in every way—lovely in colour, most subtle in the quivering expression of the lips, and sweetness of the tender face, shaken, like a leaf by winds upon its dew, and hesitating back into peace."

The brilliant Millais had risen too far and too fast to figure in Gabriel's plan. Yet he too, in that earlier summer of implacable Scottish rain that had somehow set his course to the rescue of Ruskin's neglected Effie, had wished more than once that "there was a kind of monastery that I could go to." On his wedding-day, Effie had confided to her diary, "he cried dreadfully, said he did not know how he had got through it, felt wretched: it had added ten years to his life." Drying his eyes, he had sat down to write to a close friend: "This is a trial without doubt as it either proves a blessing or a curse to two poor bodies only anxious to do their best." They seemed to be doing pretty well, and there was a baby boy. Holy wedlock, Millais was now wont to declare, was "healthy, manly and right." All the same, he caught the communal infection. His idea was to bring Effie and their baby to shack up with his beloved Hunt, on some plan that could include Hunt's sister and two other artists who were living with him on Campden Hill.

The lines crossed, it will be seen, in the person of Hunt. But Brown's Emma had made sure, in her incorrigible way, that Lizzie should have the data connecting Hunt—whom she disliked anyway—with the unmentioned, the almost unmentionable, Annie Miller. There came an evening when there was company— including Gabriel—in Lizzie's Hampstead lodging, and Brown dropped in with the innocent intention of further discussion towards the harmonious accommodation, as he put it, of "two or three married couples." The overwrought Guggums went into one of her "terrible white rages," from which Gabriel fled. And on 26 February he sent a note to Brown: "She now says that she would strongly object to the idea of living where Hunt was, of which objection of hers I had no idea to any such extent." Community projects collapsed like the house of cards that Augustus Egg was painting into the first episode of his serial domestic tragedy, *Past and Present*. And Miss Siddal, who might at this point have become Mrs Rossetti if she had known the cards better, continued to be unmanageable. Her mortal symptoms did indeed bring Gabriel to borrow £10 for a wedding, but he spent it in some other manner on his way home. And in the end means were found to despatch Lizzie to the care of relatives in Sheffield and the waters of Matlock.

If matrimony had not been placed outside the field of mere experiment, it might have had the lure of an adventurous solution. Florence Nightingale had tabled, under stress, a curious reflection:

We must all take Sappho's leap, one way or other, before we attain to her repose—though some take it to death and some to marriage, and some again to a new life even in this world . . . Popular prejudice gives it in favour of marriage.

But Edward Lear, so pleasant to know, so often unhappy to be, was expressing a widely shared male hesitation when he cried: "If one could only unmarry again if it didn't suit!—only one couldn't." So one left it to the Owl and the Pussycat, all unaware that the caul from which Frau Freud had last year unwrapped what the stork had brought to her Moravian village portended a magus.

The marriage-rate, the *Lancet* reported, was in fact falling. Social rigidity and an emphasis on prudent matchmaking produced irregular separations as well as unsanctified connections, and *The Times* declared that thousands were living in sin with little thought for the consequences. In the society where one might meet Aurora Leigh and Lady Waldemar at rout, drum, soirée or reception, youth piped its claim:

> The young run on before, and see the thing
> That's coming. Reverence for the young, I cry . . .

But there was always some maturer voice to dispose of it:

> If young men of your order run before
> To see such sights as sexual prejudice
> And marriage-law dissolved—in plainer words,
> A general concubinage expressed
> In a universal pruriency—the thing
> Is scarce worth running fast for, and you'd gain
> By loitering with your elders.

In Hanover Square, close to the fashionable wedding-church with the bronze hounds at its door, an eminent elder had certainly seen the thing that was coming, and had a mind to ease it over the threshold. Lord Lyndhurst, eighty-five-year-old survivor of two successfully happy marriages, was equipping himself by patristic studies to demolish the case advanced against legalised divorce by Bishop Wilberforce of Oxford, popularly known as Soapy Sam.

The cautious and complex Divorce and Matrimonial Causes Bill which the Palmerston administration was concerned, after long delays, to carry through in the new session, involved more than a theological skirmish. The existing situation was in itself a breach of the stronghold, since it admitted a wife's adultery as ground for divorce where the husband was prepared to go to the trouble and expense (around £1,000) of an action for "criminal conversation," a separation in the Ecclesiastical Courts, and a private Parliamentary Bill to finish the matter. Despite this, or because of it, fundamentalist argument was bound to harass the introduction of a less cumbersome and more equitable procedure. And Lyndhurst was convinced that the climate for reform had been distinctly damaged in the previous session when the Bishop of Oxford, from his place in the House of Lords, had stated that St Augustine of Hippo, though repeatedly questioned on the matter, had provided no authority for the admissibility of divorce.

In the evening of his long career Lord Lyndhurst had trouble with his hearing. But his sight had recently been restored by an operation for cataract, and his mind and memory were at full pitch for the task of digesting the Early Fathers. In due course he reached a passage in which Augustine averred: "That it is lawful for a man to dismiss a wife for that which is *stupris committitur*— that is, adultery—does not admit of doubt." Returning from the fourth century, Lyndhurst drove to the House of Lords and requested a postponement of the Divorce Bill's Second Reading to a date when both he and the Bishop of Oxford could attend. It was agreed to take it on 3 March.

IV

MARCH–APRIL
If the Comet's Coming

S O FINE HAD been the weather in London and the southern counties since mid-February that credulous persons bethought themselves of The Comet: not just any comet, such as *The Times* reported now and then as recorded by one European observatory or another, but the one which, according to Dr Cumming, was on the thirteenth of June to separate the dross from the pure metal of redeemed humanity in its wrathful furnace. The *Punch* issue of 7 March broke into verse:

> Hey! a Comet's coming, CUMMING, CUMMING,
> Ho! a Comet's coming, expected very soon . . .
> If the Comet's coming, CUMMING, CUMMING,
> If the Comet's coming, ice will be a boon.

But next morning, which was Sunday, Londoners who had repaired to church in sunshine came out into a murderous hailstorm. The temperature had fallen by nine degrees within a few minutes, and after the hail came a sudden high wind, whirling freezing sleet and snow through the streets. Four hours later there was an even fiercer squall, with huge hailstones of a peculiar crystalline formation, and then for two days and nights the snow fell heavily. At Harrow the epidemic of measles which had swept through the school in the mild weather quickly receded, and in rural Hampshire the Rev. Charles Kingsley was confirmed in his view that what passes for fair weather is in every way less healthy than a good dose of the wintry elements. The idea was worth a poem.

> Welcome, wild North-easter!
> Shame it is to see
> Odes to every zephyr;
> Ne'er a verse to thee . . .

The Rector's objection to the reading of prayers for rain or sun was partly based on his belief that the unregarded science of meteorology required to be studied as a feature of the divine system; and partly on the observation that what is good in one aspect is bad in another. But there was no disguising the association of his enjoyment of manly exercise in keen weather with his outlook on events as a Broad Church theologian. The inspiration of Carlyle had now been succeeded by a temporary phase of revulsion, and on his last visit to Cheyne Row, in November, 1856, he had kept his temper with difficulty. It was not only the prophet's "raving cynicism" which had upset him. Kingsley saw himself as "the most sensuous (not sensual) of men," and ceaselessly upheld the sacred carnality of matrimony as exhibiting —in face of mariolatry and the celibate ideal—"the distinctive superiority of Protestant over Popish nations." And to see Mrs Carlyle, who for once was braving out the winter in London, looking pale and ill, had roused him to denounce Carlyle to F. D. Maurice for his want of sympathy and attention to his wife. "Whatever her faults may be, *he* has no right to neglect her. I am sick of his present phase, moral and intellectual, though I never can forget what he has taught me."

Advanced by Maurice's Christian Socialism, Kingsley could feel in self-confident moments the mantle on his own shoulders. "I am the prophet of convulsion," says one of the characters in his well-received novel *Two Years Ago*. "I cannot cry peace, peace, where there is none. I see Christendom drifting towards the hurricane-circle of God's purpose." Nothing could maintain his own balance better than a breast-high scent in boisterous weather, with the pack well out in front.

> Chime, ye dappled darlings,
> Down the roaring blast;
> You shall see a fox die
> Ere an hour be past.

Nothing could better restore purpose to his confused and corruptible countrymen than a memory of *Westward Ho!* against the Spanish idolaters and a call to further adventure in the punishment of alien wickedness. The verses flowed from Eversley Rectory in a steady rhythm.

> But the black North-Easter,
>   Through the snowstorm hurled,
> Drives our English hearts of oak
>   Seaward round the world . . .
> Come, and strong within us
>   Stir the Vikings' blood;
> Bracing brain and sinew;
>   Blow, thou wind of God!

In London the bitter squalls lost some of their force after the middle of March, assisting John Ruskin's recuperation after one of his tiresome colds. Saturday the twenty-first was "a lovely but breezy and variable morning. Walked round garden with my mother without great coat.' It was a day of some public excitement over the mid-term Dissolution of Parliament.

The Chinese trouble was the cause of it. A friend who called upon Lord Lyndhurst one day in February found him "in high force, with the Blue Book before him, getting up the China case, on which he means to have a day in the House of Lords." Lord Derby, "the Rupert of debate" and ostensible leader of an unleadable Opposition, gave him his chance; Shakespeare ("Man, proud man," etc.) gave him his peroration on the follies and iniquities of a little brief authority; and the Bishop of Oxford, on this issue, found himself on the same side. Alone among the ecclesiastical peers, Soapy Sam stood out with a warning that did honour to his cloth:

> Remember that He who has made the sand so light and impalpable that the wind of the desert bears it away upon its wings, powerless as an element, has yet set it to be a sufficient barrier to the raging sea; that Power will, if need be, find in the weakness of China an element to chastise and rebuke the pride and strength of Britain.

The motion of protest was defeated. But what mattered, one way or the other, was the chastisement and rebuke of Palmerston. On the day that the debate closed in the Lords it was opened, on Cobden's motion, in the Commons. Everyone scented battle, the Government accepted that it was a matter of censure, and there were three adjournments—with a week-end for reflection—before it was taken to a division at two a.m. on the fourth night. Since it was essential for speakers assailing the Ministry to make their individual stands on principle and disclaim any purely political motive, their orations became increasingly impassioned. Lord John Russell, who had headed a Whig administration in the past but now had only two or three supporters, produced an unexpected pugnacity, and the thunders of Mr Gladstone, who got along without adherents, were allowed to have been magnificent. The Government, on the other hand, had resolved to support their representatives in Hong Kong over actions which their Attorney-General, behind closed Cabinet doors, had shown to be indefensible. Their spokesmen therefore intervened only to accuse their parliamentary critics of a venal conspiracy to drag down the Noble Lord's administration and substitute that evil, inchoate and unpopular thing, a coalition. As for the Noble Lord himself, his reply to the motion on the last night was reported by Greville to have been "very dull in the first part, and very bow-wow in the second."

Disraeli, unsure of his ground in any rearrangement of power at this moment, had begun by pointing out the respectable seniority of Chinese civilisation, and ended with a bitter challenge to Palmerston to go to the country on a programme of "No Reform! New Taxes! Canton Blazing! Persia Invaded!" And this, after the vote had gone against the Government, is very much what Palmerston prepared to do, leaving *Punch* to summarise the result of the debate in its inimitable fashion:

For Hauling down the British Flag, apologizing to the Chinese, and putting Derby, Dizzy and Gladstone in office	263
For maintaining the Honour of England and keeping Pam in place	247
Chinese majority	16

The authority of Lord Lyndhurst on the illegality of the proceedings at Canton had been freely quoted in the Lower House against the Government that had insisted on approving them. But in the stir of the final debate and division, which took place on the night of Tuesday, 3 March, it was hardly noticed that Lyndhurst was at the same time helping the Government in the House of Lords to carry the Second Reading of a Bill which, as the Bishop of Oxford vainly protested, "would shake everything and settle nothing," and would "tend greatly to unhinge

men's minds" in regard to "a great institution of God, upon
which the purity and happiness of this Christian land, more than
upon any one other matter, do indeed depend." The fate of the
Divorce and Matrimonial Causes Bill in the Commons was one
of the things which a Dissolution would necessarily postpone.
And it was, of course, a Dissolution—rather than a ministerial
resignation—for which Palmerston had been playing from the
moment that censure raised its head.

Such an outcome, if it had to be one or the other, would also
suit the Queen, who had been much put out by the signs of a
disturbed session at a time when her womb demanded the utmost
consideration. "The pride of giving life to an immortal soul,"
as she was to tell her eldest daughter, was all very fine, but "I
think much more of our being like a cow or a dog at such
moments; when our poor nature becomes so very animal and
unecstatic." For the twelfth time (three had died in infancy) she
was required to nerve herself for the approaching ordeal at the
hands of the royal physicians—"such a complete violence to all
one's feelings of propriety (which God knows receive a shock
enough in marriage alone)." When the China debate was prolonged she put off her intention of retreating to Windsor. But on
the morning of the final day Prince Albert had to inform Palmerston that Her Majesty's health now imperatively required her
to go into the country:

> The Queen feels herself physically quite unable to go through
> the anxiety of a Ministerial Crisis and the fruitless attempt to form
> a new Government . . . and would on that account *prefer any other
> alternative.*

The alternative was soon presented, and by the time that the
Queen signed the Dissolution Proclamation on the twenty-first,
the omens of an exceptionally crazy display at the hustings were
already apparent. Greville, shaken out of his temporary approval
of Palmerston, reacted with unwonted emotion against "the
false and hypocritical pretences upon which this dissolution has
been founded, and the enormous and shameful lying with which
the country is deluged." But the diarist restrained, as a man who
could not face the loss of friends, a sudden impulse "to write,
print and publish the truth." Gladstone, with a reasonably safe
seat for Oxford University, could afford the appearance of washing

his hands of the whole distasteful business, while lamenting in his correspondence that "we have lived into times, politically more disastrous to the honour of the country, than any we have formerly seen. For the first time is her government guided by a man without convictions of duty; by a man who systematically panders to whatever is questionable or bad in the public mind, who lives simply on the dissension of those who disapprove of his policy, and who now seems at last to have overshot his mark."

But the old gamecock himself was in capital form, first at the Mansion House when the Ministers of the Crown were banquetted, and thereafter in the address which he issued to his Devonshire constituents at Tiverton:

> An insolent barbarian, wielding authority at Canton, has violated the British flag, broken the engagement of treaties, offered rewards for the heads of British subjects in that part of China, and planned their destruction by murder, assassination and poisons.

There was substance in the outrages that made so much of his case, but he saw no reason to mention that they had followed, not preceded, the British naval action; or indeed that the villain in the Hong Kong bakery, who had long ago been caught, tried and shot with three accomplices, had spread the arsenic too thinly. A couple of hundred people had been taken ill, but none fatally. As a conspiracy, it was as ineffective as that which Palmerston was now exposing so amusingly among his floundering opponents.

Cupid was seventy-three years old, and the darling of his people, or of a sufficient number of them to give other suitors a rough time. In the mounting hysteria of the run-up to the polls many people found the newspapers totally unreadable. But across the Channel, where Palmerston was always news, the election aroused curiosity as a limited plebiscite concerned with him alone, which is roughly what it was. The author of *La Dame aux Camélias*, it was reported in England, was coming over for the *Paris Presse* to cover the spectacle of the islanders at their democratic exercises. In the view of one London editorial it would do the mercurial French no harm to be shown with what decorum a free people could declare its voice. But in fact it was Dumas *père*, not *fils*, who arrived. He knew no English, and his efforts to probe the party situation were not helped when Disraeli described the Whig Palmerston as the Tory head of a Radical cabinet. Confined to his hotel on a Sunday with nothing to do, Dumas wrote a one-act comedy and left it at that. In Kingsley's opinion the French had already discovered "that a despotism need not interfere in any wise with the selfish state of society, but that they can make money as fast under a Napoleon as under Christ"; and when the English commercial class reached the same conclusion, "Manchester will not lift a finger to save the liberties of England."

Kingsley was feeling a little wild, a little isolated from his Christian Socialist friends, who could not take his own principled stand, on China or other such questions, "as between the Englishman and the savage or foreigner." But what Manchester would do did indeed seem a prime point of interest in the elections. Its former idol John Bright, who had heard in the approaches to the Crimean War the beating of Death's wings in the House of Commons, was in Italy, and prevented by illness from returning to defend his seat. So Cobden was canvassing Manchester for Bright as well as Huddersfield for himself. As the diligent Friedrich Engels had been reporting back to Karl Marx in Hampstead, Manchester had four thousand new electors, mostly small shopkeepers, managers and so forth, who could be expected to prove loyal to Bright. The same view was probably taken by Richard Monckton Milnes, who had been urged to contest Bright's seat. For he decided to stay with his Pontefract constituency, where he rode about in the bitter weather with a feverish cold while his wife, martyred by shivering headaches, supported him from her carriage. For Bright's place the Palmerstonian contender was Sir John Potter, reputed the fattest man in Manchester—"a born alderman and a great ladies' man," recorded Engels, with "no brain but a behind all the bigger for that." In a year like 1857, and a month as mad as March, that was strong competition.

Whatever might happen at Manchester, what Marx anticipated —and with relish—was the general result of a Palmerston dictatorship over a new, passive and obedient Parliament. In the first place this would confirm his deduction that the English middle classes had been lulled by the fragmentation of parties into the slumber of political complacency. In the second place it would produce, he felt sure, "not only very welcome mistakes and complications in foreign affairs, but also very violent domestic agitation." The winter of Marx's discontent, the hopeless poverty, the bourgeois burden of private tutors for his daughters, the inherited liver-trouble, the machinations of his distant associates, the editorial chicanery of the New York *Tribune* to which he was contributing, the uncertainty of his wife's temper under the strain of another pregnancy—all began to be penetrated by the revolutionary breath of spring. "The old comic," as he called Palmerston, had no stauncher supporter.

The electoral rites went forward, the coursing season came to an end, and the hares pranced and boxed and cavorted across the fallows, displaying in their ambisexual retromingence one of the cogent reasons for believing them to be witches. In Glasgow on 23 March died Madeleine Smith's lover, Pierre l'Angélier, in considerable agony. At Stafford Assizes, on the following day, a trial was opened which gave *The Times* leader-writer a momentary break from politics:

> This is the 24th of March, 1857. Men can go to New York in ten days, and communicate with Constantinople in twenty minutes. In the opinion of everybody but the Chinese and the Pope, we pass for a very civilized and enlightened people . . . Yet on this very day, of this very year, turns up a real trial for witchcraft.

Witches, however, had been placed beyond legal peril by an Act of 1792, thus exposing Thomas Charlesworth, the owner and occupier of a forty-acre farm near Stafford, to a plague of malevolent troubles. The cheese would not "come," the dairymaids fell ill, the cows "lamented," the horses plunged and lamed each other in the stable, the dogs howled all night and a stranger-hound, "all on fire," was seen to rush through a closed door and vanish. And with all this, the victim of prosecution was the man employed by the farmer to put an end to the nuisance by his special skills. His name was James Tunnicliff, and the case attracted wide attention. It added one more symptom to the evidence of anarchic and irrational tendencies which threatened at one point or another to clog the wheels of progress.

Madness itself lay ominously in wait. The increasing pressures of life in 1857, declared Dr Hawkes of the Wiltshire County Asylum, were responsible for a marked rise in the lunacy figures, and the ultimate catastrophe was not far from his mind:

I doubt if ever the history of the world could show . . . a larger amount of insanity than that of the present day . . . It seems as if the world was moving at an advanced rate of speed proportionate to its approaching end.

The Queen was not the only one to be narrowly watched by her nearest and dearest for the recurrence of hereditary dementia. Ancestral spectres gibbered from many a cupboard. Young George Meredith, afflicted by the moods of his wife Fanny, who alternately matched her cutting wits with his and retreated into melancholia, reflected too late that there had been lunacy as well as literature in the family of her father, Thomas Love Peacock. The curse of Bowerswell had hung over Ruskin and Effie Gray, married in the very Perthshire mansion in which John Thomas Ruskin had gone mad and killed himself thirty years before. Rossetti's mother was the singularly strong-minded member of a highly unbalanced tribe, of whom one, Byron's physician John William Polidori, had done away with himself by a subtle poison of his own composition. Lizzie Siddal's childhood had been darkened by contact with a terrifying murderer.

Next to consumption, and equally vague in its apprehended doom, "brain-fever" was a familiar menace. Child-birth was one of the last areas of medicine to advance from the primitive, and the teeming wombs of middle-class homes, producing their infant-casualties with fatalistic frequency, must expect even in the surviving flock some straked and speckled members such as Edward Lear, a twentieth child and epileptic. The path to fertile womanhood was beset by hysteria, *furor uterinus*, and disturbances attributed to "tight corsets worn while reading French novels": the path to virile manhood by variously recognisable forms of nervous tension, of which the signs were earnestly considered by the sufferer and his friends. Herbert Spencer embarked upon a career of celibate devotion to rationalist philosophy with the consciousness of "labouring under a nervous disorder," his sleep perpetually broken, his days disturbed by the fear of falling into some mild imprudence from which a kindly "keeper" might have saved him, yet unable to commit himself to the remedy of matrimony which his intimates repeatedly urged upon him. The opposition of Ruskin's parents to his marriage with Effie Gray had only yielded to alarm for the health and sanity of a precious son who had confessed to them that "I cannot look at anything as I used to do, and the evening sky is covered with swimming strings and eels."

The laudanum that was to finish Lizzie and the chloral that was to finish Gabriel were carefully prescribed, with cannabis and other drugs, among considerate friends. But Charles Kingsley, in advance of the splendid salvation of his marriage, had hit upon his own cure. From the age of sixteen he had been a prey to "spectral illusions accompanied with frightful nervous excitability." But at twenty he discovered the pleasures of tobacco. "The spectres vanished; the power of dull application arose; and for the first time in my life, I began to be master of my own brain." His stammer, however, took longer to subdue. Nor did he abandon the private solace, remarked upon by a stricken acquaintance in his Cambridge days, of making drawings "such as no pure man would have made or could have allowed himself to show or look at."

But beyond the evidence of adolescent vapours and adult eccentricities loomed the starker questions framed by a *Quarterly* reviewer in its first issue of this year: "Is it a necessity of progress that it shall ever be accompanied by that fearful black rider which, like Despair, sits behind it? Does mental development mean increased mental decay?" An American authority had answered in somewhat similar terms to the Wiltshire alienist:

The press and the rostrum, the railway and the spinning-jenny, the steam-engine and the telegraph, republican institutions and social organizations, are agencies more potent in preparing the mind for insanity than any or all of those vices and casualties which exert a more immediate and striking effect.

There were more ways of going mad than by self-abuse and self-indulgence. But the *Quarterly*, while admitting the imperfections of statistical deduction, used it to arrive at one rather comforting conclusion. The Commissioners of Lunacy had stated that "patients of the middle and upper classes under confinement in private asylums" had been somewhat reduced in number over an eight-year period, notwithstanding the rise in population. But the number of pauper lunatics *appeared* to have increased over the same period by upwards of sixty-four per cent, thus proving "that it is not the intellect of the country that breeds insanity, but its ignorance, as it cannot be for one moment contended that the great movements now taking place in the world originate with the labouring classes."

It could be shown, moreover, by a comparison of figures for the rural and the manufacturing districts, that "the Hodges of England, who know nothing of the march of intellect, contribute far more inmates to the public lunatic asylums than the toil-worn artisans of Manchester or Liverpool, who live in the great eye of the world and keep step with the march of civilisation, even if they do but bring up its rear." And the idea that "mental activity was destroying the national mind" was finally, if un-gallantly, refuted by "the well-ascertained fact that the proportion of lunatics is greater among females than males."

The corollary of intellectual exercise as a form of therapy had been strikingly followed in an institution well known to Effie Gray-Ruskin-Millais and her parents, Murray's Royal Asylum at Perth, where the lecture-programme for the winter of 1856–7 read like an Athenaeum prospectus. Dr Miller, the Rector of Perth Academy, addressed the inmates on Chemical Affinity; Mr Barclay, Sheriff-Substitute for Perthshire, examined the Authenticity of Ossian's Poems; the Natural History of Man was dealt with by Dr Stirling of Perth, that of Zoophytes by Mr Croall of Montrose, and the Genesis of Thought by Dr Browne of Dumfries. Two clergymen lent their aid, one with Sketches from the History of Ancient Nations and the other on Winter, its Lessons and Associations. And there was Prof. Blackie from Edinburgh to dispose of Beauty. The captive audience offers a more cheerful spectacle than that of Ruskin's resistant critics in the world outside, declining "to be preached to death by a mad governess"; or of Ruskin himself, reflecting in a mood of disillusion that "people were never meant to be always howling and bawling the right road to a generation of drunken cabmen."

The Perth Asylum was no doubt exceptional in the range of its activities—there were concerts, balls, conversaziones, theatrical performances by the patients, a journal entirely produced by them, and all sorts of sports. But some of these things had been tried also at Colney Hatch and elsewhere, and in general the treat-ment of lunacy had made strides since the days of close confine-ment and neglect. However, there were still black spots. And the Bethlehem Hospital in London, though much improved from the infamous conditions of old Bedlam, was taken to task for "caging

Elizabeth Siddal. By Rossetti

Florence Nightingale. By J. Barrett

John Ruskin. By G. Richmond

Charles Dickens. After W. P. Frith

Distin's Monster Drum at the Handel Festival. From *The Illustrated London News*

The Crystal Palace after re-erection at Sydenham. Photograph by P. H. Delamotte, *c.* 1855

up together the coarse and the gentle, the virtuous and the abandoned." In this mixed company, behind "gratings like those which enclose the fiercer carnivora at the Zoological Gardens," there had languished for some years the gentle and gifted artist Richard Dadd. Sinking into schizophrenia under the weight of a marvellously charged imagination, he had killed his father in one of his recurrent paroxysms. Someone in charge at the asylum had at length had the sense to give him materials and facilities to paint his meticulous and elaborate visions of fairyland. The one that he was engaged upon at this time occupied him for many years and is now in the Tate Gallery.

The limitations of a rationalised approach to life's profounder problems were a trial to many philosophic minds. But as the elections drew to a close in the first week of April, they provided the kindest comment that anyone could produce upon the utter rout of Bright, Cobden and their associates. These men had risen to great influence, it was suggested, by a single academic argument for Free Trade and Peace, only to be overwhelmed by emotions that they had ignored. The punishment of their pacifism, as it seemed to Greville, had been predetermined. Gladstone and Disraeli had coasted in as expected, and Lord John Russell had won an exciting contest in the City. But Palmerston's personal triumph was undeniable, and the new Parliament presented him with a substantially increased majority. Supposing this to be accompanied by a serious opposition at last forming *outside* Parliament, Marx perceived with delight the ingredients of a major crisis which might spread, with any luck, to the Continent as well. To him at least it seemed that "John Bull's 'noble indifference'" in the revolutionary year of 1848—when the English effort had petered out in a petition taken in three hansom-cabs to Westminster through the pouring rain—was about to be handsomely avenged. It is hard to know at what point Ford Madox Brown, in the protracted story of his picture *Work*, conceived the sandwich-men winding, tiny in the distance, up the Hampstead High Street. But a keen eye could discover their message as VOTE FOR BOGUS.

The philanthropic Earl of Shaftesbury viewed the whole course of events by lights of his own. In the painful question of the China conflict he had voted with the Government in the Lords, and must there persuade himself that it had law and right on its side. "The Chinese," he told himself, "are doubtless insolent, irritating, aggressive and false. We, on the other hand, give abundant provocation in the pertinacity and outrage of our opium smuggling." Against this traffic he was waging a conscientious campaign, but having got as far as a requirement that the law officers of the Crown should consider and pronounce upon the legality or otherwise of the whole nasty business, he had a reason for keeping in with the Government in the meantime. Any threat to Palmerston's ministry, moreover, caused Shaftesbury, as a leading Evangelical, to tremble for his own influence on the Prime Minister in the vital matter of ecclesiastical preferment. Palmerston's favour for Middle and Low Church appointments, and the Queen's own distrust of High Church extremism, owed less to "Bishopmaker" Shaftesbury than was generally supposed. All the same, he could only hope that "God, having made Palmerston his instrument for good, will maintain him. But His ways are inscrutable."

Inscrutable, too, the ways of a partially enfranchised people. Unimaginable the manipulations of office. The state of parties a kaleidoscopic confusion. Convinced that there was still some fun to be derived from parliamentary business, Palmerston was frankly pleased by the disappearance of certain pious faces and tedious tongues. And the Queen, whose degrading condition was being prolonged somewhat beyond its time, took solace in corresponding, with no pretence of impartiality, with her clever Prime Minister:

> The Queen is glad to see that everything went off so well at Tiverton and that the elections are going on so famously . . . That Messrs Bright, M. Gibson, Cobden and Layard, Sir J. Walmsley, etc., should be turned out, is excellent, and very striking . . .

A reasonably deferential stability was the ideal, a House of Commons which would not whittle away at the military estimates, nor poke its collective nose into the regulation of the royal parks, nor rudely question a proper settlement for the Queen's children and a proper title for her husband, both of which issues she intended to reopen when her travail should be past.

It was 14 April, the day after Easter Monday, when at last she "was amply rewarded and forgot all I had gone through when I heard dearest Albert say 'It is a fine child, and a girl.'" A trace of qualification crept into the public rapture at what could no longer (observed the *Illustrated London News*) "be considered a novel or unusual event," even though it was of a nature to excite "the warmest feelings of respect and loyalty." But presently Viscount Palmerston was able to proffer, with his humble duty, a double felicitation: upon Her Majesty's rapid recovery and upon the presence in the new House of Commons of "more gentlemen and more men of character and substance than is usually the case."

"Safe and moderate" was another way of putting it, when the clubs had settled down again after all the excitement. It seemed as unlikely that the Ministry would substantiate Palmerston's guarded electoral references to Reform as that a helpless Opposition would find anything worth pressing to a division. Gladstone was said to be concentrating his attention on the translation of Homer, Disraeli to be saving himself for more propitious times. The conflicts with Persia and China (the world's two oldest empires, as somebody thought fit to comment) were flagrant examples of official disdain for criticism. But the former appeared to have reached a superficially satisfactory settlement, which made it (with the device of charging the expeditionary force to the Indian revenues) a war which had been entered upon, prosecuted and concluded without reference to Parliament. It was now somewhat late to take the matter into the lobbies, and the openings for more serious scuffles over the China question had been sealed off by the appointment of a mission (armed) to be conducted by the Earl of Elgin. While *Punch* portrayed Palmerston belabouring a Chinese whom he held by the pigtail, with the encouraging caption "Go on, Pam, give it to him!" the *Quarterly* drew its only considerable comfort from the idea that the victory of the late Opposition in the China debate would remain as a permanent honour to the House of Commons and "a beacon of hope and confidence to all those feebler races of mankind, with which we are in contact at nearly every point where they exist on the surface of the earth."

Somewhere between them, Greville could only view with foreboding the prospect of "wading to our ends through all sorts of horrors and atrocities, which it does not become us to inflict; though the Chinese are a savage, stupid, and uninteresting people, who in some degree deserve the sufferings that will be inflicted on them, though perhaps not at our hands." The transports and the warships went down the Channel on their long errand, and it was only in the smallest type, at the foot of some inconspicuous column, that the newspapers printed their occasional quotations from the Anglo-Indian homeward mail, with their curious accounts of symbolic chapatties ("indigestible little unleavened cakes, the common food of the poorer classes") circulating on some absurd pattern in northern India. Sometimes there was room for the correspondent's comments:

> Nobody has the least idea what it all means. Some officers fancy it is a ceremony intended to avert the cholera; others hint at treason— a view encouraged by the native officials. Others talk of it as a trifle, a joke. For myself I believe it to be the act of some wealthy fool in pursuance of a vow.

It is a relief to turn to the House of Lords, where a livelier session was promised, if only because the resumption of debate on the Divorce Bill was expected to reflect internal enmities among the Bishops on the one hand and the Law-Lords on the other. The grizzled poll of Lyndhurst would no doubt rise serenely above a sea of contentious troubles. But at this point, sitting at his table with an enormous legal folio propped in front of him, he was discovered to be absorbed under its protection with a different class of literature.

The book that riveted the veteran's attention was *Tom Brown's Schooldays*, "by an Old Boy," just out and spreading like wildfire. Its appeal to an adult readership was secured from the start by the superbly evocative description of the coaching journey, before the arrival of Queen Victoria and the railway, to deliver the new boy through dark and dawn into the keeping of Dr Arnold. Its anti-intellectual glorification of the Rugby system in its experimental stage was a contribution to what the heavier reviews liked to call the *vexata quaestio* of the extension of education to the more brutish section of the population. And the apotheosis of the dead headmaster was nicely timed for the translation of his son Matthew, by a vote of 5 May, from the Education Office to the Oxford Chair of Poetry.

But above all *Tom Brown* was wholesome. One could be sure of it from the first meditations of the Berkshire squire preparing to take leave of his young son:

> I won't tell him to read his Bible, and love and serve God; if he don't do that for his mother's sake and teaching, he won't do it

for mine. Shall I go into the sort of temptations he'll meet with? No, I can't do that. Never do for an old fellow to go into such things with a boy. He won't understand me. Do him more harm than good, ten to one. Shall I tell him to mind his work, and say he's sent to school to make himself a good scholar? Well, but he isn't sent to school for that—at any rate not for that mainly . . . If he'll only turn out a brave, helpful, truth-telling Englishman, and a gentleman, and a Christian, that's all I want.

All the same the publisher, Daniel Macmillan, was taking no chances with the tone of the thing. His first objection, before the book was completed, had been to a reference to "those whom they call atheist and infidel." "If it were changed for Methodists or Dissenters or something of that kind," he had told the author, Thomas Hughes, "it would answer the purpose and save you from giving offence to many good people." This emendation had been successfully resisted, but on profanity Hughes gave in. "As to the 'dammes'," he wrote, "I give you *carte blanche*. I can't remember above two altogether. Only mind, boys then swore abominably. I did myself until I was in the fifth." He further allowed Macmillan to substitute "inhumanly drunk" for "beastly drunk," although not without some irritation.

The purified product, at all events, struck all sorts of people as a highly moral, but not a pietistic work, indeed "the jolliest book they ever read." So Charles Kingsley assured his friend the author, in a letter breathless with the pursuit of fox and fish.

Among a knot of red-coats at the cover-side, some very fast fellow said, "If I had such a book in my boyhood I should have been a better man now!" And more than one capped his sentiment frankly . . . I remark now, that with hounds, and in fast company, I never hear an oath, and that, too, is a sign of self-restraint. Moreover, drinking is gone out, and, good God, what a blessing! I have good hopes, and better of our class than of the class below. They are effeminate, and that makes them sensual . . .

V

APRIL–MAY
Dusty Answers

———————— ✦ ————————

T HE ECLIPSE OF the Manchester school of politicians had occurred at the moment when "the rudest great town in England" (as Nathaniel Hawthorne called it) was putting the finishing touches to an unprecedented act of homage to culture. On the broad estate of Sir Humphrey de Trafford, where the Manchester Cricket Club had the use of a pitch, a temporary structure of enormous size had been erected for the Art Treasures Exhibition, and the adjacent railway-line had for months been bringing precious packing-cases to the site. Choice items of the royal inheritance had been loaned from Windsor. Prince Albert, who had fathered the enterprise and was booked to perform the opening early in May, was to display the bargains of his own eclectic taste with a Duccio and a Cranach. The great Soulages Collection, which he had persuaded the Manchester Committee to purchase outright when the Treasury declined to make a grant for it, was to be shown as a whole. In a dozen counties ducal wallpapers were patchy with the lifting of Claudes and Canalettos, the Panshanger Raphaels and the Woburn Velasquez. And the space allotted to the home product reflected the taste (to quote the *Quarterly Review*) of the new patrons:

> In their dwellings buried in the pleasant valleys of Derbyshire and Lancashire, within the shadow of the tall chimney and the rumble of the cotton-mill . . . wisely abstaining from things for which they have neither feeling nor sympathy, they have sought the works of our native schools, and have actually not hesitated to pay for a genuine picture by an English painter as much as the fashionable connoisseur would have paid for a spurious production with a foreign name.

Living British artists on a nominal roll had in fact chosen their own contributions to the Exhibition by invitation. Together with the careful grouping of Old Masters into schools and the

declared object of bringing light and knowledge to the working
population, it all sounded as if Ruskin had had as much to do
with it as the Prince. But this was not so. The two men whose
conjunction at this mid-century might have seemed fore-ordained
to fruitfulness left scarcely a sign that they were aware of each
other's existence. Ruskin's less than ecstatic reception of the
princely triumph of six years earlier in the Great Exhibition can
hardly be the whole answer. Someone—probably Sir Charles
Eastlake and his formidable wife—was doing some fencing off.

President of the Royal Academy, Director of the still embryonic
National Gallery, pillar of the art establishment and courtier
of the Prince, Eastlake's output as a painter was naturally reduced
by his promotion to great affairs. But at no stage had Ruskin
been able to admire his canvasses without considerable reserve.
Lady Eastlake, as it happened, was a close confidante of Effie
Gray. A connection was thus visible between her comments
behind her fan on the scandal of Ruskin's marriage-bed, and those
that she had recognisably contributed to the *Quarterly* in 1856
on "the qualities of premature old age" in Ruskin's writing: "its
coldness, callousness and contractions."

No doubt Ruskin had asked for it. It had been provocative to
remark, in his Academy Notes: "Hereafter it will be known
that when I have thought fit to attack a picture, the worst policy
that the friends of the artist can adopt is to defend it." But Lady
Eastlake was not a person to be under-estimated. On the avowed
principle that "something of the Ruskin is needed, at all events
in process, to catch a Ruskin," her fifty closely-printed pages of
assault on the current volumes of *Modern Painters* had been
rounded off by a clinching argument from quantity: "Only on
the wrong road could so much have been said at all." Even
for readers of a mid-Victorian stamina, the charge of over-
production against a writer still short of forty had some bite.

For art to be true to nature—whatever that might mean—
was not in Ruskin's view to be thought of as easy, "and therefore
contemptible." Turner had been volubly vindicated, the battle
of the first Pre-Raphaelites in the Royal Academy "completely
and confessedly won." But it was not the Eastlakes who had
conceded victory. They were still pointing out "examples among
the young whom we know by experience to have derived the
greatest hindrance from Mr Ruskin's works, leading them to
perverse and sophistical dreams instead of earnest action, and

instilling no principle but that of contempt for all established authority." The established authority of the Manchester Committee had decided that photography was to receive, in company so august and various, its definitive recognition as an aesthetic activity. To legitimise this offspring of Science and Art seemed to many thoughtful persons a hopeful step towards the reconciliation of its sundered parents. But was it possible, in a year of such devious possibilities, that the photographers had been invited to Manchester in the hope of confounding Ruskin's formulations on the subject of "imitative art," and deterring the new collectors in Leeds and Liverpool from their encouragement of a rebellious generation?

Artists were still, in their different ways, painting stories, and poets were still writing pictures, and photographers were preparing to move in on both. They can't supply colour, said the artists. They can't supply movement, said the writers. Wait a little, the answer might have been, and we shall supply both. We shall take over the business of illusion, and by proclaiming it as truth we shall take over that business also. At the very least it was a speculative topic of which the *Quarterly* felt bound to take note. The long and impressive essay on the new craft which it published in April, 1857, was as usual unsigned. But again it came from Lady Eastlake, and she produced some ingenious arguments to dispel an incipient alarm that man might be in the process of replacing himself by his own machines:

> The more perfect you render an imperfect machine, the more its imperfections come to light . . . The broader the ground which the machine may occupy, the higher still will that of the intelligent agent be found to stand.

Her vision of the realm which the Goddess of Photography could command reached surrealistic intimations:

> What are her representations of the bed of the ocean, and the surface of the moon—of the launch of the *Marlborough*, and of the contents of the Great Exhibition— of Charles Kean's now destroyed scenery of the *Winter's Tale*, and of Prince Albert's now slaughtered prize ox—but facts which are neither the province of art nor of description, but of that new form of communication between man and man— neither letter, message, nor picture—which now happily fills up the space between them?

Already the amateurs of the camera were devising their private *montages* from fanciful juxtapositions. At art exhibitions Lewis Carroll was making hasty sketches on the margins of the catalogue, "chiefly for the arrangement of hands." But there were two themes—the female nude and the allegory or subject-picture —which Lady Eastlake's survey had somehow failed to touch. Spurred by the opportunity held out by the Art Treasures Exhibition, a professional photographer in Wolverhampton prepared to combine them on an ambitious scale.

Oscar Gustave Rejlander, the son of a Swedish officer but English by marriage and adoption, had mastered photography as a professional aid while supporting himself as an art-student by copying Old Masters in Rome. It was two years now since he had firmly laid aside brushes and palette and converted his Midland studio for camera-portraiture and photographic services. There was good business to be done with carefully posed sepia portraits, *carte-de-visite* size or larger, of Wolverhampton merchants and their crinolined consorts. But he meant to remove himself to London, which by now supported more than a hundred and fifty such establishments, and encouraged loftier aims by regular and well-reviewed exhibitions. For Manchester he now assembled, with the help of Mrs Rejlander, some thirty separate negatives in a figure-composition, a yard broad and sixteen inches high, which imitated to the point of caricature the more pretentious conventions of academic art. With a title of a fashionable banality—*Two Ways of Life*—it presented, bang on centre, a bearded sage who was seen to be loosing two youths, in vaguely Grecian fancy-dress, on their respective courses towards separate groups of figures representing Industry and Dissipation. This latter concept allowed Rejlander to pose the undraped bodies, or nearly so, of his fancy under the licence of moral purpose and circumstantial irrelevance which was available to High Art. Even so, the idea of actuality attaching to the camera-product caused him to be accused in some quarters of indecency, and although Manchester accepted his offering, a second print which he sent to Glasgow had to be censoriously cut for exhibition.

The ultimate test of the full frontal nude was something which Rejlander preferred not to face. It had been tried out in the previous year, but for a limited circulation and in Paris, where Nader's beautiful study of Christine Roux allowed the camera a discovery only less significant than that of the distributed motion of a horse's legs. The bosky delta as a point of attention, which has been plausibly believed to have unnerved Ruskin in the person of his wife, came by curious ways to furnish a legalistic canon for an otherwise indefinable obscenity.

Rejlander had spent many laborious weeks in the concoction of *Two Ways of Life*. The painting that Ford Madox Brown called *Work* was to occupy him, on and off, through eleven troubled years. That it occupied him more than anything else during this spring was a consequence of having secured a patron in "the wondrous Plint," the Leeds stockbroker whose bounty Rossetti was glad to share with his friend. Inveigled into Brown's studio, Mr Plint had contemplated the unfinished work and the dozens of studies, while Gabriel's beguiling voice sang the praises of its creator, and its creator made gruff efforts to outline his long-pondered theme: the sun-drenched glorification of the heroes of labour digging up a Hampstead street, while the life that they sustained in its various degrees of affluence flowed placidly around them. The kindly stockbroker had warmed to the enterprise, and said he would write. Which he did:

> Could you introduce *both* Carlyle and *Kingsley*, and change one of the *four* fashionable young ladies into a quiet, earnest, holy-looking man, with a book or two and *tracts* . . . Think this matter over.

There were four hundred guineas at stake, and Brown did not take long to think it over. The irony of incarnating the Gospel of Work and Muscular Christianity as leisured spectators troubled him less than the problem of approaching either of them for sittings, and in the end it was F. D. Maurice, not his disciple Kingsley, who got into the picture of *Work*. Carlyle got there too, but in his case Brown had to operate from a photograph.

Work was the thing, the bleak necessity and the only fulfilment, at once torment and release. And especially if one had a digestion like that of Thomas Carlyle. "Dinners do nothing for me except hurt . . . 'Work, thou poor Devil,' I say to myself; 'there is good for thee nowhere in the Universe but there.'" When Harriet, Lady Ashburton, his wealthy, witty and admired friend and hostess, died rather suddenly in Paris in the early days of May, Carlyle produced a spontaneous epitaph: "Adieu! adieu! Her work—call it her grand and noble endurance of want of work—is all done!"

Jane Welsh Carlyle had eaten out her frustrated heart over Lady Ashburton. And when Monckton Milnes brought the news of the death to Chelsea, at night under a cold moon, she was grateful that he waited for the return of her husband, who was on some errand, so as to break it to him himself. In the opinion of Milnes, who was intimate with all three of them, Jane was not jealous of Harriet "in the vulgar sense of the word." The tensions had been more refined than that. It was possible for a wife to be on good terms with the lion-hunting lady, and yet to feel further from her husband when they were all in company at Bath House or Alresford than when Carlyle was wrestling with *Frederick the Great* in that upper room in Cheyne Row, double-walled against the dawn crowing of the neighbours' chanticleer, the day's intrusions of street-cries and organ-grinders, the noises of late revelry from Cremorne. "There is not in Britain," he had written to Edward FitzGerald, "a better place of work than this garret, if one had strength or heart for fronting work to any purpose."

FitzGerald was at his Persian studies, dabbing and polishing at his couplets and quatrains from Omar, writing long letters to catch the Indian mail for his scholarly crony Cowell, who had gone as Professor to the Presidency College in Calcutta. Five months earlier, at the ripe age of fifty, FitzGerald had married a lady whom in some tortuous way he had felt bound to protect. The first month of it had plunged him into melancholy, and it had not lifted now. He had taken lodgings in London for a further trial of mutual incompatibility, but he was homesick for Suffolk. He yearned after old and absent friends, and the bachelor habits so rashly set at risk. But at least he was free of Carlyle's allergy to street-cries. From his little balcony in Portland Terrace he could see the first shimmer of green upon the trees of Regent's Park, and on the pavement below him men went by with great baskets filled with primroses, crocuses, big daisies and other early flowers. The voices of their call came up to him:

> Growing, growing, growing!
> All the glory going!

"It will almost make you smell them," he wrote to Cowell, "all the way from Calcutta. 'All the glory going!'"

If the worst came to the worst for Lucy FitzGerald, as clearly it soon must, she could count on a decently conducted separation and a sufficient settlement with which to live out her blighted hopes. For Fanny Meredith there was no way but a wild escape to Wales and to Henry Wallis, the painter of a single Academy sensation, last year's *Chatterton*. "Examine it well, inch by inch," Mr Ruskin's Notes had recommended. "It is one of the pictures which intend, and accomplish, the entire placing before your eyes of an actual fact—and that a solemn one. Give it much time." What was offered to the eye—the marvellous boy, flame-haired and beautifully breeched, pallid and dead from self-administered arsenic, in the dawn-light streaming over London outside his garret-window—was an actual fact the more piercing, as one gave it time, for the apprehended element of imposture in Chatterton's reputation. But observe, if you will, this further stratagem of superimposed reality: the model from whom Wallis had painted the dead youth was his friend Meredith, the sad young cuckold in the case, for whom "no sun warmed my roof-tree; the marriage was a blunder; she was nine years my senior." Come wind of God or sunshine of Demeter, there could be no going back to *Love in the Valley*. Only forward to *Modern Love*:

> Lovers beneath the singing sky of May,
> They wandered once; clear as the dew on flowers:
> But they fed not on the advancing hours:
> Their hearts held cravings for the buried day.
> Then each applied to each that fatal knife,
> Deep questioning, which probes to endless dole.
> Oh what a dusty answer gets the soul
> When hot for certainties in this our life!

The poet has his own way with the presentation of an actual fact. The painter, possessed of the lady but sundered from his model, "contends with greater difficulties" (opines Ruskin) when he tries again with a subject from literary history. The 1857 Royal Academy Exhibition, when it opened the season in early May, included Wallis's *Montaigne*, but it drew little attention. The man remained the artist of one picture.

As for the critic, Ruskin at least had work enough, "every day, all day long, and often far into the night," to lift him out of last year's depression. That this was so was due to Turner, and Turner's elaborate will, and Turner's dissatisfied relatives, and a final parliamentary and judicial arrangement that defeated Turner's stated intentions in more than one respect, but landed the National

Gallery with the vast collection of his works and £20,000 to house and preserve them. Backed by Palmerston, Ruskin had been allowed to assume, at his own expense, cataloguing and management of upwards of nineteen thousand watercolours and drawings by the master, indifferently packed in large tin boxes. "What Turner might have done for us," he wrote at the end of *Modern Painters*, "had he received help and love, instead of disdain, I can hardly trust myself to imagine."

It would seem that Ruskin was at some delicately balanced point in the manic-depressive rhythm where the assumption of authority had to compensate the premonitory twinges of wasted effort and blunted sensibility:

> The earth is full of *lost* power . . . And when once you feel this fully (my own work has taught me this more than most men's, for no wreck is so frequent, no waste so wild, as the wreck and waste of the minds of men devoted to the arts), when once you feel it, and understand that this waste, which seems so wonderful to us, is intended by the Deity to be a part of His dealing with men . . .

Such had been his manner, a few weeks before the Academy opened, of consoling a bereaved acquaintance. And the mood seeped over into his *Academy Notes*, which were annually considered, composed, proof-revised and printed within six days, to be sold for sixpence—as near to the exhibition's doors as the janitors would permit—in lofty competition with the journalistic reviewers. That these included the wife of the PRA was well-known. "Beast as she is," said Burne-Jones of Lady Eastlake, "she is no fool." But her command of a personal column, over the signature of "Connie," enabled her to take an extra swipe at the Pre-Raphaelites through their preferred feminine types, in paint within the gilded frames or in person at the Private View: "female horrors with thin bodies and sensual mouths, looking as if they were going to be hung, or dead and already decomposed."

"Pre-Raphaelitism is spreading," noted Macaulay, who was not really interested one way or the other, but added that he was glad of it: "Glad, because it is by spreading that such affectations perish." But on Thursday evenings, whatever might be spreading or perishing, Ruskin usually managed to drop in on Topsy and Ned—Morris and Burne-Jones—and in their company hope of a certain kind was boisterous. Rossetti also, relieved of his more

baleful pressures by Lizzie's departure to Derbyshire, would turn
up in his old plum-coloured frock-coat, waving his umbrella
for the charge upon some expedition that had taken his fancy;
to the Prinseps at Little Holland House to meet poets, painters,
actors, philosophers and debutantes in social profusion; to
Regent's Park to meet that uniquely comical and self-sufficient
character, the wombat.

Burne-Jones had just landed his first commission. Plint of
Leeds was again the patron, Rossetti the eloquent go-between, a
Rossetti poem the subject which almost chose itself:

> And still she bowed herself and stooped
>   Out of the circling charm;
> Until her bosom must have made
>   The bar she leaned on warm,
> And the lilies lay as if asleep
>   Along her bended arm.

It was the background for *The Blessed Damozel*, as usual, that came
first. Nothing would do but apple-blossom, and Ned went home
to his Birmingham parents for a foray among the Warwickshire
orchards. But in the first week of May the wind of God was once
more blowing strong and chill. The easel could not stand against
it, and the petals snowed upon the ground before they could be
painted.

The wind must drop. The golden days will come. But is it
really the Blessed Damozel who presides over the ceremonies
of approaching summer, the estival festival of 1857? Could it be
rather—is it possible?—the patroness of the Great Social Evil, La
Traviata herself, the Lady of the Camellias? Those admired and
waxen beauties grew in arboreal splendour in the Nightingales'
garden at Embley. The short-sighted and eccentric Eton master
William Johnson (*alias* W. S. Cory, the poet of *Heraclitus*) kept
them upon his desk on each Purification Sunday—a white one
and a red, standing in some way for Mary and Joseph. But
Thomas Huxley's camellia was treasured, dried and faded in his
wallet, to remind him of a lost virginity. And now, on Easter
Monday of all days; with snow and sleet, of all Easter weathers,
making the streets a misery; and of all places in Exeter Hall, the
Strand Palace of Evangelical assembly, missionary enterprise,
good causes and moral uplift, an abridgment of *La Traviata* had
been sung by Madame Clara Novello, Mr Sims Reeves and other

vocalists. It was done again, on 25 April, and a full performance was promised for the Royal Italian Opera's repertory season at the Lyceum. But the Exeter Hall programme struck a note of caution:

> NOTICE: The Exeter Hall Committee have interdicted the publica-
> tion of the above performance in the form of a book of words.

Now we are getting to it. The sap is rising. The stews are steaming. The poison is at work. And the traps are set for the unwary. Talfourd's April production at the Theatre Royal in the Haymarket was the operetta *Atalanta*. It was a frivolous confection of no special merit, but Dickens missed little that the theatres and music-halls had to offer, and he was struck by the part of Hippomenes, as played by a young member of a theatrical family billed as Ellen Ternan. He was as well known at the back of the stage as in the front, and when the curtain had fallen he called at Miss Ternan's dressing-room to congratulate her. The girl was sobbing into her handkerchief, but recovered enough to explain to the kindly visitor the cause of her distress. It had been hateful and mortifying, she confessed, to have had to "show so much leg." Enchanted by her modesty, Dickens offered words of praise and comfort, and left with the warm feeling of having encountered, as he told a friend, "a most attractive and sweet little thing."

Of such is the Kingdom of Heaven, and nympholepts were no more to be found in Dickens's dictionary than in Ruskin's. Had he not appeased a jealous deity by taking his own little revenge, in the fat and garrulous Flora Finching in *Little Dorrit*, upon the failure of Maria Beadnell to preserve intact his youthful love-image when he unwisely resumed contact after the unforgiving lapse of years? Most definitely he had not. Yet here was Thackeray, virtually if not legally wifeless, sliding more or less safely into his forties: "I have passed my critical period, I think, and don't expect again to have my sleep disturbed by thought of any female." Not that it had been plain sailing. There had been dangers to his own stability, as well as the anxious responsibility of protecting his growing daughters. There was a whole area of searching experience and tormenting imagination where the successful novelist dared not trespass. While Florence Nightingale watched with scornful impatience the majority of her sex still playing like children on the shore of the eighteenth century, Thackeray looked wistfully back to an age when prose had possibilities. "Since *Tom Jones* it has been forbidden to draw a picture of a man."

In the meantime the verbal pictures that he was drawing of kings, which stuffy persons would equally have liked to see forbidden, gave middle-class audiences all over the country a sense of sturdy emergence from the dark age of the fine gentleman.

> Children do not go down on their knees to beg their parents' blessing; chaplains do not say grace and retire before the pudding; servants do not say "your honour" and "your worship" at every moment; tradesmen do not stand hat in hand as the gentleman passes; authors do not wait for hours in gentlemen's ante-rooms with a fulsome dedication for which they hope to get five guineas from his lordship.

Had the lecturer wished he could in fact have shown that all these things, or something very like them, could still happen—except perhaps in the further example of extreme obsequiousness in the Ministers of the Four Georges:

> Fancy Lord John Russell or Lord Palmerston on their knees whilst the Sovereign was reading a dispatch, or beginning to cry because Prince Albert said something civil!

His hearers fancied, but forbore to laugh too loudly, lest they in their turn should find themselves in some inverted fashion in Thackeray's *Book of Snobs*. He had yet to try the mixture upon a University audience. But when he came to Oxford in the first week of May the whole thing seemed to go splendidly. Whatever the history dons might be thinking, the lecturer's large frame was shaken with emotion and surprise over the enthusiastic response of the student-generation.

On 9 May, when it was over, Thackeray breakfasted with a friend in Lincoln College. There was one other guest, Mr Dodgson from Christ Church. Across the kidneys and eggs, the toast and Cooper's marmalade, the two disparate innocences confronted each other in a polite and cheerful conversation. Peradventure for one righteous man, or two or three, the city might be spared. But Oxford, where the dust of doctrinal convulsions still hung in the air, was kindling towards the hothouse

Brunel at the *Great Eastern* stocks. Photograph by Robert Howlett

Building of the *Great Eastern* at Millwall

The Royal Family at Osborne, 1857. *Left to right*: Princess Alice, Prince Arthur, the Prince Consort, the Prince of Wales, Prince Leopold, Princess Louise, the Queen with Princess Beatrice, Prince Alfred, the Princess Royal (Victoria), Princess Helena. Photograph by Caldesi

Distribution of the first Victoria Crosses by the Queen, Hyde Park, 26 June, 1857

atmosphere of which Benjamin Jowett was so conscious in the days of his personal reign. Matthew Arnold was girding himself to slaughter the Philistines ("with the jawbone of an ass," clerical wits could not fail to remark) from the Chair of Poetry. And Jowett himself, Master of Balliol but still denied the Greek Professorship on a suspicion of his heresy, had responded with a curiously sympathetic intimacy to the arrival of little Swinburne. In his own student-circle Swinburne seemed to George Birkbeck Hill "the most enthusiastic fellow I ever met, and one of the cleverest," reading his poems aloud with unflagging zest, convening the Old Mortality Group to discuss Hume's defence of suicide, idolising the revolutionary hero Mazzini, execrating Napoleon III, and generally preparing to come down-wind like a fire-ship among the rocking galleons of respectability.

Already the dreaming of the spires was ripe for analysis. Flushed with the success of *Tom Brown's Schooldays*, Thomas Hughes professed to be in no hurry when seeking "the prophetic sanction" of his publishers at the end of May: "What I wanted to know was whether I should go on to Oxford, etc., with some of my old characters . . ." But the tide was turning. Walter Pater would get there before Tom Brown, and burning with a hard, gem-like flame was not in the Rugby tradition. Hughes was too late with his sequel. Even if he had switched Tom to the other place in the wake of Tennyson and his Cambridge Apostles he would have had the limping Oedipus to meet, for Samuel Butler had just got there from Shrewsbury.

One way and another, it would be no more than unregenerate man deserved if the comet should erase him, and all his perverse works, in one scorching impact. Even if it should pass contemptuously out of range, the race would still be haunted by that sense of a "terrible and aboriginal calamity" of which Newman had spoken, a natural inheritance of doom and thus of hard bargaining about the price of escape or redemption. The intimations of catastrophe were in painful conflict with the optimism of material progress, but they were seldom wholesale in their application. There were always the Elect, a minority which, however small, must be large enough to include the prophet of disaster and his immediate circle. On the outskirts of Mr Prince's Abode of Love the rival canvassers roamed West Country villages, recruiting emigrants for the distant sanctuary of the Mormons; and Dr Cumming allowed for a numerous and quarrelsome population of the Chosen when he confirmed the identification of Rome with Babylon. No form of the Messianic tradition, after all, could regard with unqualified gloom a millennium associated with the reappearance of Christ. It was a deeply serious Earl of Shaftesbury who had printed on the inner flap of his envelopes the prayer "Come quickly, Jesus." And Carlyle was lapsing from his higher function when he remarked that, if Christ came again, Monckton Milnes would invite him to breakfast. The breakfasts in Upper Brook Street, select in their way, were always well attended, and Carlyle would have expected to be there himself on such an occasion.

In an enquiring age revelation was not enough, though it offered a magnificent vocabulary. The popularity of Layard's *Nineveh*, which was being "cried up and down station-platforms" along with the daily papers and Macaulay's *History*, derived largely from the archaeologist's confirmation of biblical records. There might be confusion between Robert Owen, now absorbed in the publication of his *Millennial Gazette* from Tunbridge Wells, and Richard Owen, who had named the first dinosaurs as well as dissecting the first wombat. But if so, little harm would be done to the reasonable assumption that convulsions in the past could portend apocalypse in the immediate or distant future. The precedent of the Deluge was available to all. So too, until quite recently, had been Archbishop Ussher's pronouncement upon the Creation of Man, which assumed scientific exactitude rather than poetic vision by fixing the grand event at nine p.m. on 3 October, 4004 BC. So long as nothing human was discovered— or rather identified—below the most recent geological strata, there would be people who could still cling to that assurance. For those who felt compelled to seek an alternative theory to explain the age of fossil reptiles, it was almost instinctive to discover a natural, and repeatable, catastrophe. And how else could the presumably immutable species of animals and plants in the Garden of Eden have come to be found in continents now separated?

Charles Darwin, who had begun as a catastrophist, had developed a compulsion to investigate other possibilities, despite the arguments of scientific colleagues and the objections of old Lord Stanhope, whom he liked. At Down House in Kent Darwin was only a few miles from Chevening, where Lord Stanhope, entertaining him in 1849, had addressed him heartily across the dinner-table: "To suppose that the omnipotent God made a world, found it a failure, and broke it up, and then made it again, and again broke it up as geologists say, is all fiddle faddle. Describing species of birds and shells is all fiddle faddle." With mountains of barnacles and years of fiddle faddle behind him, Darwin was in May, 1857, at Moor Park on one of his regular visits for the water-cure. A cluster of physical distresses, palpitations, visceral disturbances (Sir Arthur Keith has called it the effort syndrome) had to be kept at bay. And a letter just received— the first—from Alfred Russel Wallace in the Celebes, required decisive action. For "I can plainly see," wrote Darwin in reply, "that we have thought much alike and to a certain extent have come to similar conclusions."

> This summer will make the twentieth year since I opened my first note-book, on the questions how and in what way do species and varieties differ from each other. I am now preparing my work for publication, but I find the subject so large, that though I have written many chapters, I do not suppose I shall go to press for two years.

So after all there might be time for repentance, more time at least than Dr Cumming would allow. The seductive devil of Natural Religion had been in retreat for years. But those who turned to Tennyson and *In Memoriam* to solace the blankness of bereavement must at once encounter other devils, dragons of the prime and nature red in tooth and claw. Earnest young clergymen, out in the country with their little geological hammers and their canvas collecting-bags, came up against the terrible tables of the law:

> So careful of the type? but no,
> From scarped cliff and quarried stone
> She cries, "A thousand types are gone:
> I care for nothing, all shall go."

Beach-combing was another contemporary passion, and George Henry Lewes, determined to try his hand at popular science, had since March been pottering among the extant molluscs of the Scilly Islands. On 11 May he left these hunting-grounds for Jersey, accompanied by Marian Evans—"the infidel *esprit forte* who is now G. H. Lewes's concubine," as Charles Kingsley had called her after her critical attention to one of his books. Naturally Kingsley did not yet know her as George Eliot.

The article which Lewes regarded as the first revelation of Marian's genius had been an unsigned demolition of Dr Cumming in the *Westminster Review*. But while the angel with the fiery sword still hovered uncertainly, it was perhaps just as well for England that this unhallowed pair should keep their little distance. It would have taxed an impartial angel to estimate how much sin had in fact been erased from the book of doom when Miss Evans, having been eliminated from the game of musical beds in George Chapman's promiscuous household in the Strand, and having failed to capture the timid Herbert Spencer on the way, had extricated Mr Lewes from the consequences of an otherwise successful journalistic partnership with Thornton Hunt. These consequences can only be summarised: alienation of the affections of Mrs Lewes, and a communal production-line which added to the ten children of Mr and Mrs Thornton Hunt and the three of Mr and Mrs Lewes another three begotten by Mr Hunt upon Mrs Lewes, with a fourth now on the way.

The shame of a legal dissolution of the Lewes marriage was not to be added to this saga. Apart from the expense of the limited but cumbrous divorce procedure which Parliament was being pressed to reconsider, the first of many adulteries in the case had unarguably been condoned. The alternative for Lewes and Marian Evans was concubinage, their enjoyment of each other enhanced by a tumescent sense of social defiance. As a mulch of experience it might all have served for the somewhat free-spoken fiction that Lewes had once produced, of which Carlyle had not been the only one to complain that there was "too much love-making." But its first fruits were George Eliot and the *Scenes of Clerical Life*, in which there was perhaps too little.

For the Blackwood brothers, however, what they must watch for in their new and instantly popular serial property was the danger of excess in the George Eliot blend of realism and irony as applied to the Evangelical clergy, who had as good a claim to be shielded as their higher Anglican brethren. The latter were currently at risk from the exuberant industry of Anthony Trollope, but the version of *Barchester Towers* which reached the public in this month of May was a shade more genteel than the manuscript that had gone to Longmans. The "low-mindedness and vulgarity of the chief actors" that had disturbed the publisher had been toned down at his request by the redrafting of several passages, the deletion of "foul breathing," the substitution of "deep chest" for "fat stomach" and so on. But over the Bishop and Mrs Proudie Mr Longman still shook his head. Were they healthily imaginable, could they actually happen, in these times of ours?

At this point honesty compels us to turn to what could and did happen between certain book-covers, or within portfolios, as laid bare on 9 May in the court of the Queen's Bench. Under separate prosecutions procured by the Society for the Suppression of Vice there were arraigned before the Lord Chief Justice two booksellers charged with publishing and exposing obscene material. Hard as it may be to believe that Lord Campbell, in his seventy-ninth year and at the top of his profession, was contemplating an offence of this nature for the first time, that is the impression which he afterwards allowed to stand.

The first case called was that of William Dugdale, one of the most prolific practitioners in the field. In 1820 he had been distantly implicated in the Cato Street Conspiracy for political assassination, and he had subsequent convictions for blackmail, libel and obscene publication, with prison sentences and seizures of stock. For the dogged bibliographer his fame rests upon the zeal with which he concocted a range of wares for all tastes and pockets, pirating and cannibalising existing works, inventing dates, titles and authors, substituting chapters commissioned or written by himself, attaching salacious blurbs to relatively innocent productions and concealing the scabrous under a staid presentation. The business address that he gave on this occasion was 5, Holywell Street, which ran at that time (it has since disappeared), parallel to the Strand. In 1857 a correspondent in *The Times* described Holywell Street as "without exception the most vile street in the civilised world, every shop teeming with the most indecent publications and prints." Five other premises in the neighbourhood were occupied by William Dugdale, concurrently or consecutively, under his own name or others such as Turner, Smith, Young and Brown; and his younger brother John ran the same kind of business at three different addresses. The quarry was elusive and resourceful.

In the dock Dugdale was truculent. He claimed to have been dragged from his house and lodged in gaol for fourteen weeks without knowing what charge would be brought and what witnesses called, and he waved at the Chief Justice a volume of the latter's own *Lives of the Lord Chancellors*, demanding to read from it a passage exposing the illegality of such procedures. When he had been quietened and induced to accept the services of a counsel instructed to defend him, the case proceeded to the main charge of publishing, on three several occasions, two dozen prints of an obscene nature, in contravention of the Vagrancy Act of 1824.

The prints having been shown to the jury, Dugdale's counsel did not contest their character, but urged rejection of the evidence of publication as that of paid spies. This was true of the first witness, Henry Dodson, formerly a brushmaker, now occasionally employed by the Society for the Suppression of Vice at five shillings a time; and the only other witness was the constable who had accompanied him to the shop. The jury's glimpse of the engravings, however, had been enough, and they had no hesitation in finding Dugdale guilty. Postponing sentence till he had heard the next case, Lord Campbell directed him to remain in the dock and took up *Regina* v. *William Strang*.

Strang was a smaller catch. The defence that he was ignorant of the contents of two objectionable periodicals, *Women of London* and *Paul Pry*, and that his other wares were without blemish, made no appeal to the Chief Justice, who told the jury that it was "no excuse for him to say that he also sold *Household Words* and other publications, of a most interesting, moral, instructive and beautiful character for which the country was indebted to Mr Charles Dickens." The verdict went against Strang, and the cheap price of the offensive papers—one penny—was an aggravation.

Meanwhile Dugdale had again worked himself up. Brought forward for sentence he loudly harangued the court, at one moment defying its authority, at another imploring mercy for the sake of his two beautiful and innocent children. He wept, he cursed, he complained that he had been robbed of £3,000-worth of his books, he shouted that on peril of his soul's salvation he was innocent, and he flourished an open penknife, which was taken from him. He got one year's hard labour in a House of Correction. When Strang faced sentence he too mentioned his wife and family, besides repeating his defence. As a first offender he was given three months' simple imprisonment, but what made the day historic was its traumatic effect upon the Lord Chief Justice.

This is not easily explained. The Dugdale stocks could certainly have furnished pornography of the hardest core, and the prints that were shown to the jury may well have been all that your imagination or mine can suggest. But according to his words in court, Lord Campbell observed the nicest judicial propriety by forbearing to look at them himself. He did, apparently, inspect Strang's penny papers. But such contemporary issues of *Paul Pry* as have survived in libraries seem strangely innocuous. Any popular news-sheet with its accounts of selected court-cases would have been equally actionable, and *Women of London* was not held up as being any worse. A periodical like the *Cremorne* of the early 1850's was a very different emanation of the underground, and so was the subsequent and still notorious *Pearl*. No student of this playful subject, indeed, would describe 1857 as a vintage year. So what, exactly, had smitten Lord Campbell between wind and water? The mind must be left to boggle.

VI

MAY

Sedition and Seduction

Where does the day begin?

Among the questions that might agitate reflective minds in the uncertain spring of 1857, this had been one which seemed to defy a satisfactory solution. As early as February it had come under discussion in a corner of the *Illustrated London News*, when a correspondent in Lichfield postulated that the day is always beginning at some point or other on the globe's surface: so that an imaginary journey around the world that occupied just twenty-four hours (and who could set a limit to man's power of locomotion?) could be conceived as bringing the traveller to each place exactly at midnight by local time, that is at the moment of transition from one day to the next. Leaving his readers to digest this finding, the editor waited until April to print the contribution of "A Mathematical Tutor, Oxford," whose identity we can guess.

The heart of the problem, as it had already occurred to Dodgson some years earlier, was perceived by choosing midday rather than midnight as the time for starting and ending the journey:

> Suppose yourself to start from London at midday on Tuesday and to travel with the sun, thus reaching London again at midday on Wednesday. If at the end of every hour you ask the English residents at the place you have just reached the name of the day, you must at last reach some place where the answer changes to Wednesday. But at that moment it is still Tuesday (1 p.m.) at the place you left an hour before. Thus you find two places within an hour in time of each other using different names for the same day, and that not at midnight when it would be natural to do so, but when one place is at midday and the other at 1 p.m. Whether two such places exist, and whether, if they do exist, any communication can take place between them without utter confusion being the result, I shall not pretend to say: but I shall be glad to see any rational solution suggested for the difficulty as I have put it.

In advance of an international date-line nobody had an answer—

unless it is to be detected in the rapid rise to popularity for even-song of John Ellerton's hymn, *The Day Thou gavest, Lord, is ended*, in which the question of where exactly it had begun was dissolved in a mellifluous continuum:

As o-o'er each co-ontine-ent and island
The dawn leads o-on another day . . .

Two centuries after Sir Thomas Browne had composed himself for night's approach with the fancy that "the hunters are up in America, and they are already past their first sleep in Persia," the hundred-and-one strokes of curfew from Great Tom in Christ Church tower now closed an imperial day of such im-probable enlargement that Lewis Carroll's logic could assume a succession of globe-girdling enquiry-points, manned by the expatriate British, whose assurances as to time and day could be relied upon.

In the cantonment at Meerut, in northern India, the hour for the evening service had been changed on Sunday, 10 May, on account of the advancing hot weather, from six to seven: at which point in absolute time the English at home had just returned from their morning worship. In Meerut, as the Anglican chaplain drove to church, he encountered some men of the 60th rifles—unarmed, since they should have been in his congregation. They were supporting two of their number, who were covered with blood. Outside the church, when he reached it, was a wild confusion of carriages and horses as European families struggled to get back to what they imagined as the safety of their well-spaced bungalows. But from the direction of the city the distant cries of an advancing mob could already be heard, and thudding hooves, and many shots.

The Eurasian postmaster in Meerut, who had been looking forward to a visit by his aunt from Agra, some hundred and fifty miles to the south, decided that evening to send a private message by the telegraph-link. His opposite number in Agra repeated the message to higher authority, and a vigilant Lieutenant-Governor passed it by wire to Calcutta, to the Governor-General who nearly two years earlier had spoken at his farewell Guildhall banquet of the small cloud, at first no bigger than a man's hand, which might appear in the serene sky and at length "threaten to over-whelm us with ruin." What now lay on Lord Canning's desk was this:

Cavalry have risen . . . setting fire to houses . . . having killed or wounded all Europeans they could find . . . If Auntie intends starting tomorrow evening please detain her.

Only a little later, and a thousand miles from Calcutta, an official toiled on horseback up the winding hill-road to the Commander-in-Chief's summer residence in Simla with another message, received in Ambala from the two operators of the Delhi telegraph:

We must leave office . . . All bungalows are burning . . . Sepoys from Meerut came in this morning . . . We are off . . . Mr Todd is dead I think . . . He went out this morning and has not returned . . . nine Europeans killed . . . Good-bye . . .

Communication—instant communication, not simply accelerated travel—plays its essential part, until at last the rebels against alien innovation can be brought to lament that they are hanged by such telegraph lines as they omitted to cut. But the transforming factor of simultaneity operates as yet within separate and isolated fields. That which was so modern as to make witchcraft seem anachronistic to *The Times* can place London and Constantinople within the same dimension. East of the Bosphorus, however, the best route for the spark to leap across Asia is not yet agreed. And westwards in the Atlantic, where the marvellous cable-ship is paying out its endless coils, the omened year has even now produced a fresh sighting of the sea-serpent. Promethean man might be venturing too far:

Below the thunders of the upper deep;
Far, far beneath in the abysmal sea,
His ancient, dreamless, uninvaded sleep
The Kraken sleepeth . . .

As a star is said to exist only when its light has reached the observer—by which time it may itself have been extinguished—so an occurrence becomes an event only at the point at which it makes a significant impact. On the second Sunday of May there is thus no Indian event—nor will be for weeks to come—to compete in the mind of the Lord Chief Justice with the disturbing influence of the case of William Dugdale and his stock-in-trade, those unclean books, those inflammatory engravings.

The House of Lords had no sooner begun its business on the

following day than Lord Campbell was on his feet to ask the Lord Chancellor whether the Government intended to introduce any measure to prevent the indiscriminate sale of poisons. He must have known, and his fellow Peers must have known that he must have known, that after much investigation a Bill for this purpose had in fact been prepared. He framed the question only to proceed from it to the horror and alarm with which he had learned that a traffic in poison more deadly than prussic acid, strichnine or arsenic was openly going on. And he trusted that immediate steps would be taken for stopping the sale of publications of so pestilential a character as the trial in the Queen's Bench had exposed. All that he got from Lord Chancellor Cranworth, however, was the stock rejoinder that the law as it stood, which it was for the Attorney-General to enforce as he thought fit, was quite sufficient for the purpose envisaged.

Still, the challenge had been made, and an opportunity to pick up the soiled gauntlet flung by the Chief Justice was to present itself, in the following week, when the Lords returned to the more absorbing question of legislation for divorce. Before they could get down to business, however, the Earl of Ellenborough was on his feet with a different issue in mind. As a former Governor-General of India (he had been recalled, to his own astonishment, for insubordination and military obsession) he had a question for the Secretary of State for War, Lord Panmure, about European reinforcements for the Army in India. Her Majesty's Ministers, he was answered, had no apprehensions for the safety of the Indian dominion. But since troops that had been destined for India were being used for the China expedition, their place would be made good by four thousand recruits to be embarked for India not earlier than the second week in June, so as not to arrive at a peculiarly unhealthy time of year. That having been got out of the way, the Divorce and Matrimonial Causes Bill was taken to the Committee stage by a comfortable majority, assisted (with certain reservations) by the Archbishop of Canterbury and nine Bishops equally committed to the Government. Lord Lyndhurst (Granville reported to the Queen) "made a most able speech in favour of the Bill, but wished it to go further, and give permission to a woman to sue for divorce if she were maliciously deserted by her husband."

It was the Bishop of Lincoln, one of the four opposing ecclesiastics, who had taken Lord Campbell's point about obscenity. It was his conviction that the press reports of actions for "criminal conversation"—adulterous seduction—under the existing system constituted "the only authorised immoral publications—the only ones which the strong and impartial arm of my noble and learned Friend, the Lord Chief Justice, cannot reach." Unquestionably the "crim-con" cases, especially where they involved aristocratic or public figures, were the great staple of popular salacity. But the source of such scandalous provender would not be dried up by eliminating these actions for damages, as Lyndhurst and others proposed, nor yet by following the Bishop of Lincoln's ringing alternative:

> Place the adulterer in the criminal's dock. Let him stand in the face of the Court by the side of the forger and the burglar, who are not more guilty than he. Let the people understand that adultery is not a foible to be treated lightly, nor a fault to be compensated by a money fine, but a crime against the laws of man, as well as a sin against the laws of God.

Without restraints upon court-reporting which no Government was likely to contemplate, the evidence of human frailty must continue (as the Queen noted with distress) to furnish the literate population with material as corrupting as a French novel.

It was all very sad. Separation was sad. The sting of death— a solemn but in no sense an unfashionable or embarrassing topic— was in separation. The appeal of heaven was in reunion. Even before marriage Charles Kingsley and his chosen mate were chatting about their eventual nest in the churchyard, and celibacy by choice or circumstance was felt to make faith in survival harder to sustain. The project for establishing civil courts and laws for divorce derived its energy from a sense of the legislative shambles of the existing state of affairs—not, or not chiefly, from the strength of public demand, which most parliamentarians under-estimated. With marriage at a premium as the expression of romantic affection and the safeguard of social status, divorce promised no obvious gain in human happiness.

> But hither shall I never come again,
> Never lie by thy side, see thee no more . . .

From these two lines of King Arthur's parting speech to the erring Guinevere, Tennyson in this early summer began to build up the *Idylls of the King*. It seems odd, somehow, that he offered the couplet to Mrs Tennyson on her birthday.

Under the dome of Panizzi's great Reading-Room in the British Museum, which had just been opened (Karl Marx made a bee-line for the M4 position among the radiating desks) Coventry Patmore was doing some Arthurian research on Tennyson's behalf. It was Monckton Milnes, most dependable of contacts for a writer, who had secured a Library job for Patmore ten years before, after the poet's father had crashed with his railway-shares. "Who is your lean young friend with the frayed coat-cuffs?" someone had asked of Milnes. But things were on the mend with the snowballing success of *The Angel in the House*, Patmore's poetic celebration of domestic bliss that kept increasing like a serial novel. The bold equation of connubial with religious ecstasy which magnetised the fringe-cults of Swedenborg, Comte and Feuerbach (translated by Marian Evans) was here reflected like sunlight on the breakfast-things. Since Patmore was at this stage still a Protestant, there didn't seem to be a catch in it, and his own first Angel, Emily Augusta, combined a perfect return of his uxorious passion with the frail and fatal destiny of beauty that must die. His concept of the transfigured resumption of sexuality beyond the grave was a later refinement. By 1857 *The Angel in the House* had just reached the end of Book II, *The Espousals*, with the lines:

> But here their converse had its end,
>   For, crossing the Cathedral Lawn,
> There came an ancient college-friend
>   Who, introduced to Mrs Vaughan,
> Lifted his hat, and bow'd and smiled,
>   And fill'd her kind large eyes with joy,
> By patting on the cheek her child,
>   With "Is he yours, this handsome boy?"

We can see what the poet meant when he assured his Emily in March of this year, in a letter from Hastings, that "all that I have written in 'The Angel' about love is much below the intensity and delicacy of the plain reality."

The sincerity is not to be questioned, but it would leave no such postal evidence without the fact of separation in this life. On this Emily wrote with admirable good sense:

> It requires separation to keep up the mere romance of love ... We
> shall fancy the romance is gone whenever we have been together
> 12 months; whereas a week's parting will bring it back directly.

The Carlyles present an extreme case. But it would not be a case
at all, or one too incredible to intrigue, but for the wry tenderness
of Thomas's letters, from a comfortable distance, to his Goody,
his Necessary Evil; and their mutual trumping of each other's
headaches; and the nervous vivacity, barbed but protective,
of Jane's responsive style. Now that she was in Scotland again,
and he in Chelsea alone with *Frederick the Great*, he must be kind
to the dog Nero and remember to care for the canaries, and not
imagine himself inconsolable.

> If you could fancy me in some part of the house and out of sight,
> my absence would make little difference considering how little
> I see of you—and how preoccupied you are when I do see you.

It is rather reassuring than otherwise to know that in Scotland
there was a gentleman who, though likewise bound to another
partner, cherished for Mrs Carlyle a continuing and reciprocated
love.

Larger than life, walking relays of friends off their feet and
acting his own creations off the stage, there was enough of Dickens
to run a two-ring circus. A wife, ten children and a sister-in-law
were being moved into Gad's Hill Place with the same brisk
attention to detail that ordered the disposition of the furniture and
the supervision of the water-supply. The literary engine that met
the mounting and meticulously kept accounts would have been
cruelly worked by any normal standard, but this one was chroni-
cally overcharged. With *Little Dorrit* disposed of at last there
was a head of steam to be dealt with. "I am quite confident I
should rust, break and die if I spared myself." That was the way
to answer the anxious attempts of Forster to restrain him. But
Forster was down on the horizon. Wilkie Collins, younger and
cheerfully dissolute, was in the ascendant, abetting a dangerous
tendency to brood on lost springtimes of imagined happiness.
Perhaps it was this change of influence that goaded Dickens
into self-pitying revolt against the pattern of family propriety
that had been the deliberate background for the play of his
literary genius. But that would be to overlook the near approach
of the expected comet, and the month's sudden turn from a falter-

ing and tantalising spring to a warmth that was either a premature high summer or the first confirmation of the fiery prognosis of Dr Cumming. May was at its most genial when Dickens told Collins that "any mad proposal you please" would stimulate "a wildly insane response." And again:

> If the mind can devise anything sufficiently in the style of sybarite Rome in the days of its culminating voluptuousness, I am your man . . . If you can think of any tremendous way of passing the night . . . do. I don't care what it is. I give (for that night only) restraint to the Winds.

With no record of what voluptuousness, if any, the adult mind devised, we return to the schoolroom where innocence struggles tediously to construe the sybarite classics. From Harrow windows the wandering attention of the boy Symonds dwelt on the still delicate green of trees in full leaf, and in the unclouded distance "we see every speck on the plain from Sydenham to the far-off Surrey hills, with Windsor, Hampstead, and Elstree." The weather, he reports to his sister in his Sunday letter of 17 May, is *melting*.

> Never—not even last August—have I felt so oppressed. I very nearly fainted in church. It has been a tiring day—I heard three sermons including Dr Vaughan in his ponderous style . . . I think the nights are the worst part, where you fry and then go on to be stewed in School for breakfasts by a morning sun which beats in. I never, however, saw this place looking so pretty . . . I have divested myself of all the clothes I can.

Long walks with his chum Alfred Pretor. Long sermons from Dr Vaughan. And no thought as yet of the double-tongued serpent basking in the shade in this ambiguous Eden, waiting to corrupt them both. Speech Day is on the second of July, and the holidays begin on the twenty-eighth. Seventy-one summer days to be crossed off.

> Alas, that Spring should vanish with the Rose!
> That Youth's sweet-scented Manuscript should
>   close!
> The Nightingale that in the Branches sang,
> Ah, whence, and whither flown again, who
>   knows?

Nearing the merciful end of his six-month marriage, Edward FitzGerald had taken a house at Gorleston, near Yarmouth, almost within hail of George Borrow, who had just sent him the two new volumes that he called *Lavengro* ("with some excellent things and some very bad, as I have made bold to write to him—how shall I face him?"). Leaving his wife at Gorleston, Fitz-Gerald made off on that hot Tuesday, 19 May, to talk about Hafiz with a friend at Hertford; and bungled trains, as he often did, and found himself at Bedford; and there read the news that his Hertford acquaintance had died suddenly on the very day of their appointment; and repaired therefore to the comfort of a much closer friend, in a Bedfordshire country house with a pleasant garden, and a paddock for the horses.

> I put away almost all books except Omar Khayyam which I could not help looking over, in a paddock covered with buttercups and brushed by a delicious breeze, while a dainty racing filly came startling up to wonder and snuff about me.

Seasoned with English meadows, the letter-packet for Cowell went off to Calcutta, steaming in its half-imagined heat and its unimaginable apprehension. It was FitzGerald's fancy to render Omar's verses for his distant friend in a quaintly monkish Latin, in which the Persian New Year, reviving old desires, became the return of Earth's Golden Age.

All the glory going, while another incurably bookish bachelor-spirit contemplated his only enemies, "those execrable dandelions." Macaulay's library at Holly Lodge opened upon a sloping lawn, with two elms, a willow and a mulberry, and bordered with flowering bushes and standard roses, "my little paradise of shrubs and turf." But the view from his bedroom, he wrote playfully to his youngest niece, affronted him with dandelions:

> The day before yesterday, when I got up and looked out of my window, I could see five or six of their great, impudent flaring, yellow faces turned up at me. "Only you wait till I come down," I said. How I grubbed them up! How I enjoyed their destruction! Is it Christianlike to hate a dandelion so savagely? That is a curious question of casuistry.

That done, he could relax in the enjoyment of a Maytime more delicious than he could remember ever to have felt and seen. "The lilacs are now completely out; the laburnums almost completely. The brilliant red flowers of my favourite thorn-tree began to show themselves yesterday. Today they are beautiful. Tomorrow, I dare say, the whole tree will be in a blaze." And after that the rhododendrons that he had put in on Christmas Day, in the first enthusiasm of his arrival on Campden Hill. "In three or four summers, if I live so long, I may expect to see the results of my care."

Whether anyone except the elect of God would live so long was still, for the susceptible, a matter of concern. But Robert Owen, in the evening of his long and extraordinary life, was not prepared to give the last word on human affairs to a comet. In his eighty-seventh year he gave notice that his Congress of the Advanced Minds of the World would be held in London from 15 to 24 May, "to consider the most practical means by which gradually to supersede the existing false, cruel and most ingenious system for the government of the world, and to establish for ever the true and good system in spirit, principle and practice." Organised in a businesslike way at two central assembly-rooms, the advanced minds applied themselves, in those ten suddenly sultry days, to a succession of topics from money to spiritualism, producing for all who cared to attend a full explanation of the principles and practices, "as certain as the law of nature," whereby permanent peace and happiness could be secured for the earth's population. The objection that for Christians the way to this millennium had been set forth in the Gospels had been anticipated. It could be shown that at the First Coming of Christ the time was not yet ripe for expounding to the undeveloped nations of the earth a practical system of universal love and charity.

That time had now come. The Satanic Age was confidently declared to be over. But, all the same, it was getting very hot: *enormously* hot, they said at Epsom, where the going for the Derby had seldom been known to be so hard. Blink Bonny won by a neck in a cloud of dust and a lather of sweat, and went on to win the Oaks as well. Only by *Punch*, it was claimed in Bouverie Street, had the Yorkshire-bred mare been tipped, months ago, as a Derby winner. Mr Frith, who was not a racing-man, had made some studies at Epsom in the previous year, and could get anything he wanted of the 1857 meeting from the camera-work of Robert Howlett. He therefore remained in his London studio,

G

diligently progressing with the Dickensian passages of the *Derby Day* stunner with which he proposed to beat the field and stupefy Mr Ruskin at next year's Royal Academy. Mr Dodgson, who was not a racing-man either, had studied the Derby odds as given early in May; and from Oxford he had sent to the editor of *Bell's Life in London and Sporting Chronicle* a letter to demonstrate the mathematical certainty of making a winning book by taking odds in the proper proportion. The paper did not publish his letter, but answered it in print: "Your theory looks well enough on paper; the difficulty would be to find backers to work it out." And Dodgson then discovered from a friend that his system, already known in sporting circles as "betting around," was considered an ungentlemanly practice. More to the point, its profits were too marginal to repay the trouble.

Fell influences were at work, and the unoffending were not immune. On 17 May, that melting Sunday of the three Harrow sermons, Dodgson had as usual walked back to the Christ Church Deanery with the Liddell children after morning service:

> I find to my great surprise that my notice of them is construed by some men into attentions to the governess, Miss Prickett . . . And though for my own part I should give little attention to the existence of so groundless a rumour, it would be inconsiderate to the governess to give any further occasion for remarks of this sort. For this reason I shall avoid taking any public notice of the children in future, unless any occasion should arise when such interpretation is impossible.

Alas, is it ever impossible? But in a summer such as this the Lord of Misrule can hardly dispense with Lewis Carroll. Nor yet with Edward Lear, from whom a signal, dated 1 May, had been sent home from Corfu for decoding:

> I am coming to England fast as I can, having taken a redboom at Hamsens 16 Upper Seymour Street, Squortman Pare, and also a rorkwoom or stew-jew at 15, Stratford Place.

His movements were not really very fast, but before the month was out he was in London. Flustered to find himself so busy that he ought to go to seven hundred and fifty-six places every evening, he disappeared for a three-day visit to the Tennysons at Farringford, and then to Nuneham near Oxford, one of the

four superbly hospitable mansions (the others being at Dud-
brook, in Carlton Gardens, and the neo-Gothic fantasy built
by Horace Walpole at Strawberry Hill) of the spectacular Countess
of Waldegrave, twice widowed, inheriting both fortunes, and
now married to the suitably rich and colourless Mr Harcourt.
A dream of Trimalchian affluence to inaugurate a cornucopial
season, meloobious voices floating from candle-lit alcove to
starlit parterre, the heady scent of *Bottlephorkia Spoonifolia* and
Manypeoplia Upsidownia. But when *They* said "Is it nice?" a fellow-
guest could only report: "I have sat with old Lear both nights,
he in low spirits, longing for 'sympathy,' which means a woman,
specially a wife."

Calling up the faery reserves, London journals let it be known
at the end of the month that Hans Christian Andersen was shortly
expected on a visit to England as a guest of Charles Dickens.

THE FIRST OF JUNE was Whitmonday, and gloriously fine. The doors of the Great Oven were opened for the crowded excursion-trains to stream off the happy slag towards field and heath and sea. One traditional outlet for saturnalian enjoyment had recently been closed by authority, and the abominations of Greenwich Fair must fade into a tolerant past. But the down-river paddle-steamers were as busy as ever, loaded now with sightseers for the *Great Eastern* on its Millwall stocks; and the hostelries along the Greenwich shore greeted a prosperous summer with tuns of ale and millions of whitebait. For Londoners, said the *Illustrated London News* between full-page engravings of Brunel's growing prodigy, "the launch will be—unless the Comet interposes—the final and crowning glory of the season."

In Regent's Park the Zoo had nearly twenty-three thousand visitors. Passing to and from the tunnel under the carriage-road, or turning sated from the refreshment-room and the monkey-house, some at least must have paused at the wombat's modest address, now renumbered 46 in the helpful guidebook. On the first, almost unnoticed arrival of the pair who had succeeded the original female, they had at once dug themselves in, and for some time they would only emerge at dusk for their food. By 1855, however, when their portraits appeared in James Gould's *Mammals of Australia*, care and flattery had produced a gratifying response. "They not only admit the closest inspection," reported the artist, "but may be handled and scratched by all who choose to make so intimate an acquaintance with them."

Upon their own intimacies, however, they drew a veil of proper discretion, so that though they had bred once and might hopefully do so again there was no certain knowledge as to how they set about it. Richard Owen, the greatest zoologist of the day, could only surmise that the procedure resembled that of the kangaroo, for whom coitus "is of long duration, and the scrotum during that act disappears, and seems to be partially inverted during the forcible retraction of the testes against the marsupial bones."

The matter might be dismissed as one of idle or indeed offensive curiosity, but for Dr Acton's reliance in his pioneering sex-manual on examples from the animal kingdom. It is true that he did not cite sickliness or delusions in monkeys as a consequence of masturbation, but his graded approach to the sexual functions and disorders of the highest created being provided lessons that could be readily grasped. Ignoring the birds and the bees, he quoted Rymer Jones on the hermaphrodite snail ("at length, having received the love-inspiring wound of this singular weapon, the smitten snail prepares to retaliate"); and Richard Owen on the spider ("the young and inexperienced male—always the smallest and weakest of the sexes—has been known to fall a victim, and pay the forfeit of his life for his too rash proposals"). The "prolonged copulation of the dog" was set in contrast with that of stags observed in Richmond Park, where "the act is accomplished in an instant, and the female retires, to be replaced by another." After a series of such excursions Dr Acton could feel that "the perusal of the preceding pages must have convinced my readers that the male receives a great amount of pleasure from the copulatory act." To convince them that the human female is differently constituted he had only to remind them of the feline caterwauling that disturbed the Londoner's repose:

> Few, perhaps, are aware of the cause. It arises, I am told by those who have watched the animals, from cries during the act of copula-tion. The noise proceeds from the she-cat, and arises probably from the torture she experiences.

Transferred to the human context of the teeming city it was enough to give anyone the shudders. But it was Acton's com-passionate object to allay a different and debilitating dread, the fear of "so many young men . . . that the married duties they will have to undertake are beyond their exhausted strength." The trouble, as he saw it, began with a school curriculum anchored to "Lemprière's Classical Dictionary with its filthy stories of the loves of the Heathen Mythology." Ideas of feminine avidity tended to be confirmed by the sowing of wild oats (for even Dickens confided that he would think something was wrong with any son of his who delayed to dispose of his chastity). Impressions of a strongly reciprocal passion (which the novice might not suspect to be counterfeit) derived from "association with the loose women of London streets, in casinos and other immoral haunts," might bring the reckless youth to the marriage-bed with alarming visions of the permanently devouring female. The *vagina dentata* had not yet been identified by anthropologists, but the physician had seen enough to persuade him that there were powerfully erroneous notions to be countered. "The best mothers, wives, and managers of households" could be trusted to be quieter than she-cats in making known their reactions to the whole business. But with the reassurance that they "know little or nothing of sexual indulgences" Acton added the weight of his authority to the vaguely acceptable confusion of class with species.

These were arguments too nice for an avenging Comet. As the halcyon days lapsed in fiery sunsets towards the combustible Thirteenth of June, the jests and rumours of common conversation took on a certain edge. In popular pulpits the resolve to give no countenance to secular heresies fought a losing battle with the impulse to turn the theme to good account. In the popular press it was hard to distinguish between apparently reliable meteorological items and unattributable snippets about patent flameproof clothing and the like. The forward planning of London hostesses was hedged with half-serious caution, and the announcement that a long-running play would be performed "positively for the last time" on the thirteenth (which was a Saturday) drew an unusual amount of comment. Those to whom crossing oneself remained unthinkably superstitious found in these days a great deal of wood to touch.

Aloof to panic promptings, the legislature seemed at the same time sharply divided, as between Lords and Commons, in the spirit with which it faced the inscrutable future. The torpor of the Lower House was such that Disraeli, with no intention of disturbing it himself, foresaw a short and easy session. To his friend Mrs Brydges Williams he wrote airily on 7 June:

A philosopher who laughs at the theological view of the question, and therefore shocks the ladies, has, however, frightened them equally by his scientific announcement that the world has already been destroyed 27 times; that, reasoning by analogy, it must be destroyed again, and probably often; that he rather imagines it will not be destroyed on the 13th inst; but there is no reason why it should not be destroyed before that, as the destructive agencies are all rife—in the centre of the earth a raging fire, while the misty tail of the Comet would, if it touched us, pour forth an overwhelming deluge—so that in 4 and twenty hours we may be shrivelled or drowned. In the meantime, if the catastrophe do not occur, we hope to be at Torquay by the end of next month.

But in the other Chamber, as one report put it, "there must be some unknown stimulant, some legislative and oratorical philter in the body politic of their lordships" to account for their "galvanized vitality." Could it be the return of the colourful Lord Brougham, bursting with elderly health from his annual sojourn as the uncrowned king of Cannes, and pausing on the way in Paris to give a dissertation on the differential calculus? Or were the peers indeed working to avert a cosmic doom upon an imperfect society?

Brougham, at all events, pitched zestfully into the Report stage of the Divorce and Matrimonial Causes Bill, to attack the provision allowing a wronged husband, but not an errant wife, to remarry. So far from discouraging adultery, he maintained, this would make it impossible for a seducer to be penalised by having to marry the woman. "How often," he exclaimed with feeling, "have men been checked in their course of invading their neighbour's bed by the apprehension that they might be tied for life to the victim of their seduction, whom the laws of honour would cast upon their hands!" The Bishop of Oxford's objections to the clause, and indeed to the Bill as a whole, emerged at this point as a theological reading of the Acton Effect. "The temptation to sin," he told the House, "assails the man and the woman on two opposite sides of their character. In the man the great temptation is the gratification of appetite, but it is not so in the woman." But he was no fanatic—it was his judicious flattery of both sides in certain controversies that had earned him his nickname of "Soapy Sam." And he would not have gone so far with Acton as to recognise "love of home, children and domestic duties" as the *only* passions felt by a good wife. He preferred to quote Coleridge: "The desire of the man is for the woman; the desire of the woman is for the desire of the man."

On the same warm afternoon the pioneering measure to regulate the sale of poisons, and reduce the facility with which they could be obtained with intent to murder, was safely steered into the hands of a Select Committee. There were difficult points to be resolved, such as the recommendation of soot, among other substances, as an indicative admixture. This had caused the Earl of Hardwicke to wonder how the gentlemen of the Leicestershire Hunt would look with their boot-tops cleaned with a mixture of oxalic acid and soot. But Chief Justice Lord Campbell, whom the Bill so nearly concerned, was already calling attention once again to those other poisons, as destructive to the mind as these were to the body. On that very day, he reminded them, he had presented a petition to their Lordships from the Society for the Suppression of Vice, praying that this hideous abuse might be halted. But once again the Earl of Ellenborough intruded with his different anxieties. His mind fixed always upon that Land of Regrets where for two dizzy years his word had been law, he had been brooding over incidents of disaffection reported earlier in the year from Calcutta. The notion of similar trouble in the well-garrisoned station of Meerut was, he felt, rather extraordinary, since "the officer who commands that Division has the means of putting down any mutiny in half an hour." But an indication that the greased cartridges agitation had had to be dealt with among the native cavalry in Meerut had reached Bombay by telegraph, and England by the Overland Mail—overland, that is, between the Red Sea and the Mediterranean and between Marseilles and the Channel. Ellenborough spoke his mind at some length, and with a sideswipe at Governor-General Lord Canning. Granville demolished him. "I do think," he said severely on behalf of the Government, "that there is considerable inconvenience in bringing questions before Parliament based merely upon telegraphic information."

With an equal disdain for alarmist rumour, the Queen and her husband drove to Royal Ascot, at the head of eleven four-in-hands, in brilliant sunshine. Their eldest girl's fiancé, the young Prince Frederick William of Prussia, had arrived to join the large gathering at Windsor. And on Saturday, the last day for earthly pomp by the calculation of Dr Cumming, the open carriages rolled again, all the way to London for a playing of *Richard II* in Charles Kean's renowned season at the Princess's Theatre, which ravished nearly everybody by the splendour of its costumes and crowd-effects, the vast elaboration of its scenery, and—sardonic critics reported—its occasional passages from the text of Shakespeare. Helmuth von Moltke, the Prussian officer in attendance on Prince William, sent back long and informative letters to his wife. "A Sunday in London," he began on 14 June, "is by no means a cheerful prospect; but, as the earth has not come to destruction at the proper moment to avoid it, we must just endure it."

A Sunday in Windsor—Survival Sunday—in beautiful weather, "the sky almost transparent, with here and there slight streaks of high vapour"—ought somehow to have been endurable. True, the Castle's sanitation smelt somewhat of the Middle Ages, its tapestries had been dimmed by smoky winter fires, and because of the large number of guests Moltke had been given accommodation less convenient than he remembered from a former visit. But the view from his window in the Norman Keep was certainly *groszartig*: to one side the Long Walk of Windsor Park, the roofscape of the town immediately below, and towards the other hand Eton College and the still lovely valley of the Thames. And after all, he was not locked in. The numerous Ascot party had already dispersed, the Queen kept her family Sabbath, and for the Prussian Prince's entourage there were no duties beyond the obvious one of matins in St George's Chapel. Curious about Anglican worship, Moltke timed the prayers at about one hour, "in the course of which both clergyman and congregation alternately speak." As a consequence, "one passes about half the time on one's knees, which seems an easy task, seeing that one is provided with a good velvet cushion and an easy chair at one's back, but in other respects it is really a chastisement."

The peaceful Sunday afternoon gave the future Field-Marshal a chance to recover from the ordeal of worship. With only a groom to unlock such gates as he might encounter on the royal estate, he rode at will, starting up pheasants, hares and rabbits but scarcely disturbing the herds of fifty or sixty stags and hundreds of deer, too lazy in the golden sunshine to do more than stagger a few paces from his path. His ride took him to Virginia Water and thence to Cumberland Lodge and its great conservatories: the famous vine spreading for a hundred and thirty-six feet under glass; the smaller vineries bearing ripe Muscatels and blue Hungarian grapes by the hundred, with strawberries, beans, peas and pineapples flourishing indiscriminately below them; and the greenhouses full of ripe cherries, plums and peaches. At dinner that evening he found himself placed next to the Queen. "It is so nice that she speaks German."

To some of her subjects this was not the most attractive of

Victoria's accomplishments, and her faithful Commons had uncivilly declined to sanction without comment the financial provision for a British Princess Royal to marry a Prussian heir-apparent. What the Queen had first had in mind was a dowry of £80,000, an annuity of £10,000, and a prospective measure or package-deal for meeting the needs on maturity of her other children—now by the grace of God, and as far as she knew and hoped, fully mustered. What she had finally to settle for was £8,000 a year for the Princess, a dowry cut by half to £40,000, and no prior commitments for the rest of the family.

The further question of her husband's title, which for seventeen years the Queen had been wont to underline as *of the greatest importance*, had been considered too delicately controversial to be placed before Parliament while the allowances were being exposed to vulgar discussion. And the Cabinet now discovered constitutional objections to the involvement of either Government or Parliament in any formal conveyance of royal status to the man whose hand had for so long guided the royal signature. The most essential point, Palmerston soothingly informed Her Majesty, could nevertheless be secured by Letters Patent issued under the royal prerogative and published in the *Gazette*. The Queen gave in. From 25 June, Prince Albert would be known, in communications to the public and in petitions to the Almighty, as His Royal Highness the Prince Consort.

Clearly it would be a season of distinction. With one daughter to baptise and another to exhibit as nubile, the passing of an aunt (the Duchess of Gloucester) was not suffered to cast too deep a shadow of Court mourning. It was on the stamina of the living that everything depended; and the opening test of the year's receptions, called Drawing-Rooms and held in St James's Palace, had been stiff enough to send a chivalrous tremor through the House of Commons. What ought to have been a pleasing and agreeable duty, Members were told, had become a painful and distressing task by reason of the total inadequacy of the arrangements. A function which in former days had involved only a couple of hundred ladies at a time must now cope with upwards of a thousand, attended by perhaps half as many gentlemen: "the flower of the British people, who on State occasions contribute to form the most brilliant Court in the world, and an assemblage of beauty, the like of which no other nation in Europe can boast."

Out of this throng, to take a case in point, two hundred and sixty-four ladies had got as far as being presented to the Queen on Saturday, 6 June. But all had to enter and leave by a single narrow corridor running from the main entrance of the old Tudor palace. The large room in which they had to wait their turn, familiarly known as "the pen," was furnished with wooden benches, so disposed that "they did the duty of traps and pitfalls, and caused not a few ill-fated ladies to be thrown violently to the ground." The survivors having been presented to their Sovereign, there was the final prospect of a long wait in an open shed, exposed to the weather, the near contact of inferior attendants, and perhaps the jeers of common onlookers, while a wild confusion of transport was sorted out.

> On Saturday last too many ladies had to endure all this—yes, prostrated with fatigue, fainting from the exhaustion, the heat, and the pressure of this "middle passage"; with, perhaps, costly and splendid clothing crushed and utterly destroyed—many sunk on the . . . soiled and coarse matting that covered the flagstones, to wait there in patience for the moment when the carriages should be brought to their relief.

If Asiatic hordes imagined that the flag on the Lucknow Residency would be hauled down to spare the ladies, they had evidently picked the wrong opponents.

The Commons, however, had been assured on the previous day that "the late disaffection among the troops in India had been put an end to, and any such occurrence would in future be put an end to, by the exhibition of the same promptitude and with the same vigour." For the sufferers in St James's Palace salvation depended on the enlargement of the accommodation. This was conceded by the popular First Commissioner of Works and Buildings, Sir Benjamin Hall, presently to be immortalised by Big Ben. But the plans, he added, were not as yet drawn up.

For the most conspicuous bang of an exploding season some credit must go to a Mr Distin, who had found a skin large enough to cover a drum of seven feet in diameter, fit for the gigantism of the Handel Festival that marked the re-erection at Sydenham of the Crystal Palace. Every day for a week, and for five hot hours (though with a break for refreshments) the slur upon the music-loving instincts of the British was answered under the immense glazed firmament by "one hundred and fifty first violins, fifty counter-basses, a powerful organ" and, not to mention the monster drum and its supporting artillery, "two thousand male and female singers, who were placed in eighty ascending rows." Estimates of the daily audiences, at tickets from half-a-guinea to two guineas, varied between twelve thousand and forty thousand. There could be but one shadow, nicely expressed as "regret that Handel had not lived to hear his music done such justice to as they felt quite sure it never had before been."

The royal day was Wednesday, 17 June, when nine carriages proceeded to Sydenham with an escort of cavalry along what was still, for most of its length, a pleasant country road. The weather continued fine and clear, and Moltke could not fail to be impressed by the opening of the concert:

> When the Queen entered all present rose, and *God save the Queen* was sung, the first verse coming from one single voice accompanied by the monster organ. Clara Novello sang, and filled the whole of the immense room with her voice, so that every word could be understood. Next the second verse was sung by three male voices with instrumental accompaniment, and lastly the third verse by the whole choir. Endless thousands of cheers. The Queen acknowledged by bowing repeatedly and low, only after which Prince Albert, the Archduke and Prince Frederick William came forward.

That done, however, the Prussian aide found the *Maccabeus* oratorio very slow going, and his uniform felt tight.

> The redeeming feature about the whole thing was the very excellent luncheon after the first, and the splendid March in the third act— *See, the conquering hero comes!* This melody is just as much national as is *God save the Queen*, and used to be played every time the Iron Duke entered a ball-room.

Right opposite the royal box, in a tizzy of rapture (on another day, when the *Messiah* was sung without the Queen, but that did not matter) sat Hans Andersen, with the Dickens family:

> It was like Aladdin's Palace, or rather like a fairy town, with glass streets, flowers and statues in the whole building. Beautiful lotus, red, blue and white, were growing in the broad marble canals. The music sounded so strangely that my head whirled—I almost wanted to cry. Outside the fountains were playing. It was as if we were in Undine's kingdom. Never, with the exception of the Blue Grotto, have I seen anything more fairylike.

Strolling among the fountains after the concert, watching the "many little crinolined monsters reeling before the spray," the enchanted Dane forgot the solemn beginning of the day at the nearby Norwood Cemetery, where he had attended with his host and hostess the funeral of the journalist and playwright Douglas Jerrold. Jerrold had died with shocking suddenness and his interment was on an expensive scale—pointedly so, for his family had been more astonished than pleased by Dickens's precipitate announcement that he was organising a subscription for their relief. It was a treacherous impulse, an obtuse and wombat-like gesture, an invitation to the fatal influences stored in the summer sky.

But for Hans Andersen nothing reigned in this hospitable household but "the spirit of true amiability." Except that the well proved to be dry and another had not yet been found, Gad's Hill Place had been established with furious energy as a perfect country home, less than an hour from London by rail and beautifully sited in the Garden of England. "We have children of all ages," Dickens had told him, "and they all love you." That the boys had been given such whimsically literary names (Henry Fielding, Alfred d'Orsay Tennyson, Sydney Smith, Walter Landor, Edward Bulwer Lytton) only added to the happiness of staying with a great fellow-writer. Dickens was a natural host, and Kate was his "charming *châtelaine*." There was an evening on the grassy top of Gad's Hill when they all watched the sun go down in a calm sky over the winding river, and a full moon come up; and the claret-cup was passed from hand to hand, and Andersen's own cup of happiness was like to overflow. But he knew little English, and his efforts to express to his kind hosts the magic of this waking dream made them doubt, at times, even his command of Danish. From Tavistock House, the centre for all arrangements to introduce the visitor in metropolitan circles, Dickens at length confided to a friend that "we are suffering a good deal from Andersen."

> The other day we lost him when we came up to the London Bridge Terminus, and he took a cab by himself. The cabman driving him through the new unfinished street of Clerkenwell, he thought he was driving him into remote fastnesses, to rob and murder him. He consequently arrived here, with all his money, his watch, his pocket-book and documents in his boots—and it was a tremendous business to unpack him and get them off.

Fairyland had after all its lurking dragons, its spectral temptations, its mopping and mowing shapes of evil. Nor did its hereditary guardians in the Palace of Westminster, singly or collectively,
relax their grapplings with a tainted society simply because the
Comet had passed without mischief and unseen. On the morrow
of that respite the intentions of Lord Campbell were revealed
in the First Reading, on 15 June, of his Bill to Prevent the Sale
of Obscene Books, etc. Next day it was the Marquess of Westmeath, chipping in with a reforming measure of his own, and a
petition from the magistrates of Ramsgate to support it.

It was not that what habitually took place at Ramsgate and at
Margate was worse than the case of other seaside resorts. It was
simply, as the Marquess explained, that these places were more
frequented, on account of their situation, by what he might call
a fluctuating population. At this season of the year, he continued,
it was the practice for women to go down to the sea-bathing
places and "dance in the water, without any covering whatever,"
to the disgust of the respectable inhabitants and visitors; and he
thought that it was high time for their Lordships to interfere
by way of legislation.

Their Lordships thought otherwise. Some of them may have
found it difficult to revise a mental picture of beaches monopolised
by the curtained bathing-machines from which, when they had
been drawn by horses a short way into the water, the muffled
occupants were extracted by coarse-looking viragos in mob-caps
and shapeless linen costumes, to be briefly dipped in the ocean
and then replaced. Others may have heard, as a matter of jest,
of male affronts to decency within sight of the promenading
ladies, a situation on which the Westmeath revelations could be
thought to improve. But most of them agreed with Earl Granville that the only effect of the proposed measure would be to
bring legislation under ridicule. Resolved in the negative. Dance
on, ye nymphs of Margate and of Ramsgate, to the confusion of
magistrates and the glory of the foam-born goddess. For the
doom is not yet.

The June temperatures climbed steadily into the eighties and
stayed there. Meteorological influences, *Punch* reported, had their
effect upon the senators as upon everybody else. As for "Sapona-
ceous Samuel of Oxford" (*Punch* was given to anti-clerical fun)
the Bishop did himself no good with his "canting professional
protest" when the Lords, on the twenty-third, finally sent the

Divorce Bill down to the Commons by forty-six votes to twenty-five. His last stand had been a staunch reiteration of his belief that the measure was contrary to the law of God, contrary to the law of the Church of England, and one which would be fruitful in crime and misery to the people of England. In passing it they would be dealing a more fatal blow to family purity than they could by any other act. But they passed it. "In about a year," *Punch* suggested with elephantine sarcasm, "you will hardly meet such a thing as a man with a wife."

Two days later the balance was publicly redressed by the antique ceremony of the Dunmow Flitch. The custom of awarding a flitch of bacon for the best-attested local example of a long and harmonious marriage had only recently been revived by W. Harrison Ainsworth, who specialised in popular historical fiction, and on 25 June the small Essex town was *en fête* for the picturesque proceedings. Mr Ainsworth, naturally, was there for the fun and the feast, and naturally his Town Hall speech must touch upon the "grave and perplexing questions of divorce agitating our legislators." They were seeking, he stoutly affirmed, "to lighten the matrimonial ties instead of to undo them."

For Lord Campbell the Divorce Bill, as wrangled into shape in the Upper House, represented the overdue transfer of the whole business to judicial hands, on terms broadly framed by an earlier commission over which he had been proud to preside. As against opponents who on the one side rejected divorce for any cause as contrary to Divine Law, and on the other wanted it to be available, on proof of adultery, for either partner without distinction, the Chief Justice was himself disposed to appeal to a superhuman tribunal:

> I think the true principle is, that the marriage ought only to be dissolved when it is impossible for the injured party to *condone*, and that Divine Providence has contributed an essential difference in this respect between the adultery of the husband and the adultery of the wife.

But just now he had other fish to fry. The difficulties of regulating the sale of poisons (England, Scotland and Ireland, for instance, had each its separate pharmacopeia) were being diligently ironed out, though too late to save Pierre Emile L'Angélier, whose ex-mistress Madeleine Smith was composedly facing her trial in Edinburgh, fixed for the last day of June. In the mean-time, on the twenty-fifth, Campbell launched upon the Lords his crusading bid for statutory powers to purge the body public of the poison of obscene books, prints and publications.

He was safe in assuming that not even his worst enemies in the House could do other than applaud the objective of their noble and learned Friend. He knew that Lord Chancellor Cranworth and others were satisfied with the operation of the Common Law as it affected this misdemeanour, and would prefer not to investi-gate the messy practices of spies and informers by which it had to be sustained. He realised that he would have to be emphatic to get legislation for the issue of magistrates' warrants upon affidavits of the existence of contaminating matter, and for police powers of forcible entry, search, seizure and arrest. But although his own figure as a compiler of books was a matter of ambitious concern, his more relaxed hours were blamelessly nourished by the novels of Scott, Dickens and Thackeray. Returning in maturity to Fielding and Smollett, the favourites of his youth, he had been startled to find that "their coarseness is much greater than from my recollection of it I could have imagined." And what he could not now imagine, after a sketchy introduction to the lurid wares of Holywell Street, was that any well-regulated mind should find difficulty in drawing the line.

But old Lord Lyndhurst, whose mind was better regulated than most, knew his man. As Lord Chancellor thirty years ago he had started Jock Campbell on the climb to eminence which could now be seen in a patronising and slightly ironic light. If the Chief Justice were determined to venture out of his depth on another hot afternoon, his amusing predicament should be made clear as a warning to others. Suppose, said Lyndhurst when his turn came on the motion for the Second Reading, that a policeman, under the proposed measure, has seen in a shop-window what he conceives to be a licentious print, has described it to a magistrate and obtained a warrant:

The officer then goes to the shop, and says to the shopkeeper, "Let me look at that picture of Jupiter and Ant*iope*."

"Jupiter and what?" says the shopkeeper.

"Jupiter and Ant*iope*," repeats the man.

"Oh, Jupiter and Ant*i*ope, you mean," says the shopkeeper; and hands him down the print. He sees the picture of a woman

Carlyle under the summer awning in his Cheyne Row garden,
1857. Photograph by Robert Tait

The Frozen Deep. Dickens as the dying Richard Wardour, with his daughters and Georgina Hogarth in the female parts, in the first private production in Tavistock House. From *The Illustrated London News*, January, 1857

Ellen Ternan (*centre*) as Dickens first saw her in *Atalanta* at the Haymarket Theatre. From *The Illustrated London News*

stark naked, lying down, and a satyr standing near her with an expression on his face which shows most distinctly what his feelings are and what is his object.

The informer tells the man he is going to seize the print, and to take him before a magistrate. "Under what authority," he asks; and he is told: "Under the authority of Lord Campbell's Act."

"But," says the man, "don't you know that it is a copy from a picture by one of the most celebrated masters in Europe?" That does not matter; the informer seizes it as an obscene print. He asks if the shopkeeper has got any more prints like it.

"Oh yes, I have got several others," is the answer. Whereupon the officer searches the shop, and in so doing perhaps he stumbles upon a print of the story of Danae. There he sees a naked woman lifting her eyes to heaven, but standing in a very strange attitude, the shower of gold descending upon her, a little Cupid peeping over her shoulder, pointing with his dart, and other circumstances which I will not describe.

Well, is this print also to be brought before the magistrate? These prints come within the description in this Bill as much as any work you can conceive. And yet they are both celebrated pictures. The first is a copy of a famous Correggio which hangs in the large room of the Louvre, right opposite an ottoman, on which are seated daily ladies of the first rank from all the countries of Europe, who resort there for the purpose of studying the works of art in that great gallery.

Here and among the carved nymphs and satyrs to which he briefly turned, Lyndhurst was luring the Chief Justice on to unfamiliar and treacherous ground. "I do not know," he next proceeded, "whether my noble and learned Friend's extensive reading has made him familiar with the poems of Rochester." Was he aware that "one of the principal characters in one of Congreve's plays is Lady Wishfor't?" and that Dryden translated Ovid's *Art of Love*? Lightly tossing in a few lines from *Sigismonda and Guiscardo* as a specimen, the venerable sophisticate displayed Dryden as a full candidate for Campbell's *Index Expurgatorius*, to be followed by "the whole flight of French novelists, from Crèbillon *fils* down to Paul de Kock . . . And when my noble and learned Friend's Bill is passed, every copy of them may be committed to the bonfire with as little mercy as were Don Quixote's chivalry books."

At this point Lyndhurst sidestepped to recover his guard. Certainly he deplored the existence of an infamous traffic. But it could be dealt with by the proper application of the existing law, while the proposed one would be unworkable. By the time he sat down after moving his amendment, he had tormented Campbell into attempting another speech, in infringement of the normal procedure. Lyndhurst quietly, and other voices loudly, called him to order. Standing his ground in the rising hubbub, the Chief Justice snapped out a complaint that Lyndhurst, "in his zeal for these filthy publications," had himself "gone entirely wrong as to what was the rule of the House."

It was a hot one to aim at a man who had thrice held the office of Lord Chancellor. But there was something hotter—too hot, it appeared, for Hansard to report. Preserved by his deafness from the full affront, Lyndhurst was told by officious friends, before he went home to dine, just what had been flung at him by Campbell: who with no less solicitude was privately warned that he had better apologise if he wanted to keep a single friend in the House. The Chief Justice thought it over, and later in the evening drove to Hanover Square and sent in his card. A well instructed servant, who knew the distinguished visitor perfectly well by sight, held up the card to read the name before informing him that his Lordship did not wish to be disturbed.

We must leave it to simmer. For the sun which Lyndhurst had suffered to go down upon his wrath rose next day, with the promise of another scorcher, upon the first of the multitudes flocking to Hyde Park for an occasion which it would be churlish to overlook. The military parade for the Queen's presentation of the first Victoria Crosses to sixty-two Crimean heroes of all ranks went off without a hitch, unless we are to believe the story that the first of the awards was by oversight pinned clean into the unflinching recipient's chest. Twenty thousand people had applied for seven thousand tickets to the special stands, and even Earls were among those disappointed, though there was also a roped enclosure from which the parade could be watched without leaving one's barouche. Riding in the royal cavalcade as it approached from the Green Park, Moltke was surprised that the police along the route were unarmed, and impressed by the orderliness of immense and loudly cheering crowds, who "showed also very much interest in our own stately prince." The Queen wore a scarlet and gold military habit with the Garter sash, a dark blue skirt and a little plumed hat, very becoming. The pale grey roan that she rode behaved through all the excitement with such composure that a whisper went round that it had been drugged.

Four thousand cavalry, Guards and Hussars, made a brilliant spectacle in the sunshine as they passed the saluting base, followed by a slow march of infantry, in which Moltke noted particularly the goat-mascot of the Royal Welch and "one regiment of Scots without breeches, headed by the bagpipes." Then the artillery came past with fourteen guns at a gallop, "making such a roar and a thunder," as one lady reported, "that we wondered we still lived afterwards."

It was Prince Albert's first public appearance with the title of Consort. It was General Wheeler's last day of sacrificial defiance in the entrenchment at Cawnpore, the name that still meant nothing. It was Friday, 26 June, and working up over most of England to the hottest week-end for twenty years. In the still warm evening, in his house in Piccadilly, the Prime Minister composed a letter to be carried over to the Palace with the day's despatches:

> Viscount Palmerston is sorry to have received the accompanying account of the extension of the Mutiny among the native troops in India, but he has no fear of its results . . . It will, however, seem to be advisable to send off at once the force amounting to nearly eight thousand men, now under orders for embarkation for India; and when the despatches arrive, which will be about the middle of next week, it will be seen whether any further reinforcements will be required . . .

There was no ripple to be expected from Parliament or the newspapers until Monday, and on Saturday and Sunday the shade temperature touched eighty-eight degrees Fahrenheit. The Queen took a party to Richmond and Twickenham, spending amiable hours with the season's international set in their charming villas, basking among green lawns river-lapped and cedar-shaded. Her subjects spread out from London in a hot and happy tide, to the pleasures of a siren-haunted coast where the bathing-machines and the whelk-stalls throve on summer's bounty and the restraining hand of the Marquess of Westmeath remained paralysed. Not so the finger of Fate, which late on Sunday evening vindictively nudged to disaster a crowded homeward train on the North Kent Railway.

But the fairies were looking after Hans Andersen, who was

booked for a London visit from Gad's Hill on the following day. "Indeed," he wrote to Denmark, "it was on this very line— twelve passengers perished with above sixty injured. There will be a great loss by way of compensation, but I was whimsically told that these accidents will not be stopped until they shoot a few directors."

VIII

JULY

Profligate Summer

<hr>

"JUNE OVER! A thing I think of with Omar-like sorrow. And the roses are blowing—and going—as abundantly as ever in Persia . . .

> I long for wine! oh Saki of my Soul,
> Prepare thy Song and fill the Morning Bowl;
> For this first Summer month that brings the Rose
> Takes many a Sultan with it as it goes."

FitzGerald lingered in Suffolk, waiting for the blighted bud of marriage to drop quietly from its stem, assuaging his loneliness by long despatches to Cowell in Calcutta, picturing a landscape that the exile's eyes would drink. "It is said there has not been such a flush of verdure for years; and they are making hay on the lawn before the house, so as one wakes to the tune of the mower's scythe-whetting, and with the old perfume blowing in at open windows."

Elizabeth Siddal lingered in the Peak District, attending ladies' art-classes in Sheffield and posting back to Gabriel her bitter-sweet verses. Jane Welsh Carlyle fled north at last to the native comforts of Haddington and Edinburgh, by the economy of a cheap excursion-train which her husband, as soon as he had seen her off at Euston, began to regard with mild twinges of remorse. "Oh men, men," mused Jane, "how stupid you are in dealing with us poor eggshell wretches!" But the extreme steps to which Miss Madeleine Smith had been driven (as the prosecution confidently made out) made Mrs Carlyle feel quite ashamed of being a Scotswoman: and the more so when she was told that a number of Glasgow merchants had raised £9,000 in token of sympathy for "this cockatrice." One man had given a thousand. "He had better marry her," said Jane, "and get poisoned."

On 9 July the Edinburgh High Court produced the sensational

verdict on three charges of administering arsenic or other poison
in cocoa, coffee or other article of food or drink to the late Pierre
Emile l'Angélier. Not Guilty on the first charge, Not Proven on
the other two. The widely published details of the trial, and of
her own person and demeanour, had already presented Miss
Smith to the Rossetti circle as a considerable stunner. It went
without question, said Gabriel, that the lady was not for hanging.
The equations of beauty with morality were silenced, and in the
end the lady was to reward this support by joining the twilit
London colony of artists' models.

July blazed its challenge to the painters, charging leaf and
brick and wing and petal with an enamelled brilliance that must
be seized before it should cool. Slender as a lily in his own right,
Ned Burne-Jones was painting the sheaf along the Blessed
Damozel's bended arm, from exquisite examples plucked in the
garden of Red Lion Square. He had been having his ups and
downs, Gabriel reported, but added: "I hope he's getting round—
not in the wombat sense, however—that seems far off indeed."
Darting down to Oxford on that warmest of week-ends at the
close of June, Rossetti had impulsively taken Morris with him
to meet his architect-friend Woodward.

The Long Vacation had begun, scattering the student-population,
blowing Dodgson, rather glumly, out ("I have learned almost
nothing, taught not much more, and forgotten a great deal");
and blowing Thackeray, rather oddly, in, to contest a Parliamentary by-election. The country-wide success of his lecturing had tempted this foible. But in Oxford it had been a mainly
student audience that flattered him. Its City electors might not
be disposed to embrace a literary regicide, still less a London
profligate who could declare himself at the Mitre in favour of
Sunday opening for the Crystal Palace, the British Museum, the
National Gallery, and even concert-rooms and theatres. Cornered
on this issue, he tried to reduce it to a matter of vague modifica-
tions such as would "make many people more friendly to the
clergy," promote "happiness and union among the families of
the poor," and yet not offend "the feelings of every Christian
man." But it was just enough to turn the scale against him, and
by a narrow margin his self-destructive impulse was frustrated.

In an Oxford contest of a different significance Lord Palmerston,
one might say, had been defeated. The Prime Minister's firmly
personal line on the new Government buildings for Whitehall,

turning down Gilbert Scott's Gothic competition-entry and
insisting on a Renaissance style, had been reversed in Oxford
by the triumph of Venetian Gothic in Woodward's ornate
Natural History Museum and his new building for the Union.
It was for this that John Ruskin and Dr Henry Acland, his friend
from undergraduate days, had tirelessly conspired, and the first
week in July brought Ruskin on a visit of inspection. He lodged
outside the town at Cowley, in a farmhouse with a garden of
gooseberries and orange lilies, and around it a loose wall covered
with stone-crop, and around that nothing but fields. Here Ruskin
wrote every morning until half-past twelve, then walked at the
height of the sun the two-and-a-half miles into Oxford, for a
meal with Acland and a lesson in brick-laying from the workman
who was building a study for him. The arbiter of architectural
revival could feel himself to be following his stern habit of
"doing the thing with my own hands till I know its difficulty."

Rossetti, with Morris in tow, was also on a visit of inspection.
Procrastinating as usual he had lost, both for himself and the
wombat, the chance of contributing to the designs of "crocodiles
and other vermin" which Ruskin wanted his chosen artists to
supply for the Irish masons working on capitals and borders
for Woodward's Museum—together with flowers, fruits, owls,
monkeys and the grotesqueries primly deplored by an academic
critic as "the unnecessary introduction of cats." But the other
building, the new Union, did have room on its walls for wombats.
If it came to that, there was room for the Arthurian cycle. The
Jovial Campaign, as Rossetti was to call it, was already an idea
when he and Morris took the train back to London.

Like the larger neo-Gothic vision of Ruskin and Acland, the
idea was genuine, enthusiastic and intrinsically doomed. The
quality of Rossetti lived as much in the sparks he could ignite
in others as in the wavering flame of his own creative spirit. His
poetic presence continued to brood over whatever remained of a
movement which even the *Athenaeum* was now prepared to
patronise. Of the original Brotherhood the prodigious Millais
had made his pact with popularity, respectability and fortune;
and Holman Hunt was ploughing his own, at present rather
barren, furrow. Privately Ruskin hinted that Millais had been
seduced by the worldly Effie. Publicly he had cleared himself
of personal rancour by continuing to praise Millais' work after
the domestic scandal, until the 1857 picture of the year, *A Dream*

of the Past (or *Sir Isumbras at the Ford*), drew from him the long and sorrowful piece which ended:

> A time is probably fixed in every man's career, when his own choice determines the relation of his endowments with his destiny; and the time has come when this painter must choose, and choose finally, whether the eminence he cannot abdicate is to make him conspicuous in honour, or in ruin.

Rossetti's point of decision was simpler. All that he had to do to open a fresh chapter was to accept the homage of the new young men. For covering the bare walls of Woodward's hall in the Oxford Union, which might be thought to require a close experience of the techniques of mural painting, all that was really demanded was that devotion to art as a gaily defiant activity which—like the Dada movement which it anticipated by seventy years—could despise permanence as a *bourgeois* concept.

Behind this happy rout plodded Ford Madox Brown, Gabriel's first teacher and most long-suffering friend. Cold-shouldered by Ruskin, and never strictly a Pre-Raphaelite, it was Brown who had organised their first and only exhibition for June of this year. The £42 he had spent on it from his own pocket came back with painful slowness in subscriptions from the others.

While Hampstead High Street drowsed in the summer glare, Brown added one persevering detail after another to the crowded and claustrophobic morality of *Work*, financed by the good Mr Plint with monthly instalments of £25. In the first week of July the studies for the workman mixing mortar, the pet whippet in its unseasonable jacket, the loose earth beside the excavation, a lantern and the little girl's pony, were brought to various stages of completion. Beside the mortar-mixer there was to be a poorly dressed girl, seen from behind, with a baby looking over her shoulder at the spectator. For this Brown had begun to paint the head of his infant son Arthur. But Arthur fretted and sickened, and his father rubbed out what he had done. Within a week the child was dead, and Plint had to be asked for an advance for the expenses of burial. The ghoulish prerogative of selection from the records allows it to be added that Mrs Marx's child, to her husband's relief, was born dead, and that young Mrs Beeton's firstborn of May lived only three months. "I see difficulties," a friend wrote to her on 21 July, "as regards publishing a book on Cookery. Cookery is a Science that is only learnt by Long Experience and years of study, which of course you have not had."

Brown had a painting among the Art Treasures in Manchester, but it was skied. There were disturbing reports that the northern collectors were switching to orchids, but Plint would buy it in the end. The royal stamp on the whole great enterprise had been set for the last day of June and the first of July, when Albert would return as Prince Consort, with the Queen and a suitable following, for a State entry into the cotton-metropolis and an acknowledgement of its cultural atonement.

Before the royal train pulled out of Euston on the Monday afternoon, the newspapers had spread through the kingdom the first really alarming news from India. The Queen's views about immediate reinforcements for India, and their replacement at home to the fullest establishment voted by Parliament, had been sent to Panmure for transmission to the Prime Minister. "If we had not reduced in such a hurry this spring," Her Majesty added severely, "we should now have all the men we wanted." As the train emerged from smoky urban tunnels into the green and open country, the House of Lords was being lectured by Ellenborough on the sins and errors of "a Government in India actuated by that spirit which has characterised them since I left it—a spirit which has led them to desire to obliterate all traces of my having ever existed in that country." In the Commons it was Disraeli who asked the questions, finding it odd that after the nation had been hustled into action in China and Persia to preserve the majesty of its name, it should awake to find "that the ancient capital of Hindustan is in the possession of our insurrectionary and rebellious troops."

Outside the House, however, Disraeli greeted the news from India with a jocular confidence in General Anson, the Commander-in-Chief, whose recapture of Delhi was expected to be announced in the next mail to arrive. Among his other accomplishments the General had been singularly successful with cards, and reputedly the best whist-player in Europe. "He had seen the Great Mogul so often on the ace of spades," quipped Dizzy, that he could be counted upon to know how to deal with him. "All the world laughed very much, and Mrs Anson sent off the joke to the General." Alas, he had by then been dead for more than a month, struck down by cholera as soon as he descended from the Simla heights.

By the evening the royal excursion, after a halt for refreshment at Tamworth and the passage of that grim industrial landscape which the Queen was wont to deplore, had reached the hospitality of the Earl of Ellesmere, Lord Lieutenant of the County Palatine of Lancaster, "a young, most delicate man" (observed Moltke) whose new and magnificent Worsley Hall "with its Gothic windows, doors and projections produces upon one a most decided impression." So did the next day's ceremonial events, and the self-discipline of the Manchester multitudes, although this time the Prussian noticed some exertion on the part of the police.

> One can easily see that the populace have been accustomed for centuries to govern themselves. At the same time it would not be correct to assert that all this is done without any interference whatever on the part of the police. I believe there must have been fully five or six thousand policemen on duty, each with a short staff in his hand, with which he can give the transgressors a very expressive hint. But no police could possibly restrain such a mass of persons unless they themselves also assisted.

Despite a sudden thunderstorm and the inconceivable dislocation of a civic banquet—at which Moltke, with empty wine-glasses, was served only with some fowl, followed immediately by strawberry jelly—the two-day visit was a memorable success. The Queen, after examining the wealth of art-treasures of every description and of many periods, purchased as a gift for the Prince Consort Mr Rejlander's audacious photographic composition of *The Two Ways of Life*.

London had also had its thunderstorm, but it was fine and sunny again when the Queen returned on 2 July. She had a date for the fourth of the month with Charles Dickens, who had earlier in the year been given some discreet hints of a royal interest in *The Frozen Deep*. With the Douglas Jerrold Memorial Fund as a pretext, Dickens had flung himself into a revival of that gripping drama for public performance at the Gallery of Illustration in Regent Street, where he had also established an office and committee-room for the Fund. A request through the proper channels that the Queen might help the cause by attending a performance had received the proper answer that Her Majesty could not bestow her attentions on an individual memory. She would very much like, however, to see the play, which could perhaps be done for her in Buckingham Palace. To the astonishment of Hans Andersen, to whom the idea of even the greatest of writers negotiating with his sovereign was unheard of, Dickens now demurred on a point of his own protocol: "I should not feel easy as to the social position of my daughters at the Court under such circumstances." Would the Queen relieve him of that rather obscure difficulty by coming to the Gallery of Illustration on a private night of her own, bringing her own guests?

She would and she did, attended by the King of the Belgians and some fifty other exalted people, who "cried and laughed and applauded and made as much demonstration" as anyone could expect of a small audience. They stayed until well after midnight, for the Queen had no mind to miss the farce of *Uncle John* that followed the emotion and suspense of the main offering.

Nothing could stop Dickens now. Manchester, in this proud and fateful year, must see *The Frozen Deep*. Dates were fixed for the latter part of August, the Free Trade Hall booked: and that, he decided, must mean the engagement of professionals for the female parts. The hall would be too large, the strain too much, for his own girls. Spending busy days between Tavistock House and the Gallery of Illustration, dashing off letters and articles, correcting proofs in polar costume while awaiting his cue, Dickens had less and less time for Andersen, who had virtually invited himself in the first place and showed no signs of concluding his visit. For the bony Dane, as the family now called him, the sun-drenched bliss of Gad's Hill, with or without his admired host, was not lightly to be relinquished:

> There is a fragrance of clover, the elder-tree is in blossom and the wild roses have an odour of apples, so fresh and strong. In the meadows the hay stands in stacks, and inside the house all is happiness . . . Their family life seems so intimate. Mrs Dickens is so gentle, so motherly, quite like Agnes in *David Copperfield*. The daughters are pretty and unaffected, and seem very gifted and good. He is very busy with his theatrical performances, and he went to London again this morning. However highly I may place him as an author, I must praise him just as highly as an actor in tragedy, as well as comedy.

But which was it to be?

As the Queen explained to Uncle Leopold of the Belgians, India was "*the* place where every one was anxious to place a son."

Tennyson and Dickens were no exceptions, and Walter, the eldest of the seven Dickens boys, was due to sail from Southampton on 20 July for the East India Company's military service. He was sixteen, and the parting might well give his father the feeling as of "great teeth drawn with a wrench": but not, at this point, any undue nervousness about disturbances which would presumably have been summarily repressed before the boy had a chance of winning his spurs.

Public anxieties were at present divided by the respective advocates of sail and steam as the most expeditious means of trooping to India. The Earl of Cardigan, deflated veteran of the charge of the Light Brigade, assured the Lords that steam was now the thing, but in both Houses questioners were told that the arrangements for despatching most of the reinforcements under sail had already been made and would not be changed; that the passage should reasonably be made in seventy days, and that steamers would probably take longer because of coaling-stops. No instructions, it was further learned, had been sent out to empower the Government of India to divert from their proper destination the troopships now on their way to China.

As it turned out, Lord Canning had on his own initiative been able to reach Lord Elgin, when his expedition touched at Ceylon, with this very proposal, to which Lord Elgin instantly agreed. But another idea was mooted on 7 July by the Member for Bristol, who enquired of the Prime Minister whether the Government would support the application to the Sultan of Turkey for sanctioning the construction by M. Ferdinand de Lesseps of a ship canal across the Isthmus of Suez. Palmerston was in his jauntiest form that day:

> For the last fifteen years Her Majesty's Government have used all the influence they possess at Constantinople and in Egypt to prevent that scheme from being carried into execution. It is an undertaking which, I believe, in point of commercial character, may be deemed to rank among the many bubble schemes that from time to time have been palmed upon gullible capitalists. I have been informed, on what I believe to be reliable authority, that it is physically impracticable, except at an expense which would be far too great to warrant any expectation of any returns.

It was not that he minded investors getting their fingers burned if they ignored his advice. But the political consequences would be hostile to British interests by facilitating the dismemberment of an Ottoman Empire for whose preservation so much blood had been spilled in the Crimea. As for "remote speculations with regard to easier access to our Indian possessions," the rival undertaking of a railway-connection between Alexandria and Suez would be infinitely more practicable.

What was assuredly and physically impossible, with things as they were, was the receipt of any intelligence from India, public or private, during the fortnightly intervals between mails: which intervals were nonetheless enlivened by the circulation of lurid and catastrophic rumours. Tribulations under a burning sun became the more imaginable as the warm days succeeded each other with only minor breaks. Dickens was beginning to feel desperate about the water-supply at Gad's Hill Place, where only the men employed for boring, at a combined wage of two pounds per day, seemed to relish the situation. In the nostrils of Lord Campbell, meanwhile, the summer stench of Augean stables was becoming overpowering. Rising on 9 July to address the Lords, he held in his hand a volume which would give them some notion of what was going forward.

The book, he explained, was a translation of one of the novels of the younger Dumas. It was called *The Lady of the Camellias*, and the opera of *La Traviata* was understood to derive from it. In this work, he went on, the lady described her red camellias and her white camellias in a manner which trenched upon modesty —but he would not shock their Lordships by going further. He understood that the book was sold at all the railway-stations; and he had to add that it contained thirty-two pages of book advertisements, embracing about a hundred publications, most of which were of a very abominable description indeed.

Warming to his theme, the Chief Justice had next to refer to a work of a still worse character, but this time he was not going to gratify either his audience or the publisher by naming it. It was one of the filthy publications which he believed were offered for sale in Holywell Street, and its price, which had formerly been one guinea, was now three shillings and sixpence. It was evident that Lord Campbell, who had supported the extension to the less wealthy of provisions for divorce, was not prepared to add pornography to the bounty.

Lord Lyndhurst was not in the House on that Thursday. He had retired for a few days to his country place in the Chilterns, where the full bloom of his roses had replaced the early splendour of those dubious camellias. Apprised by his friends that Campbell was whipping up some bishops for a bid to rush the measure through, he agreed to return to town on the following Monday. There was a general desire among the Lords to watch the old stag locking antlers with his challenger, so debate on the Third Reading was broken off. On Monday, with Lyndhurst in his usual seat (a special bar had been fitted so that he could support himself when rising to speak) Campbell got to it again, beginning with a communication that he had received from the Society for the Suppression of Vice.

At first glance the operations of this zealous body did not suggest a permissive climate. In a hundred and fifty-nine prosecutions which it had instigated during half a century there had been but five acquittals, prison-sentences had averaged eight months, and in early cases there had also been the pillory. The Society claimed, however, that the offences brought to its notice had been ten times as many as the proceedings which its funds would allow. As an indication of the stocks held by the lucrative trade, a windfall of 1845 gathered from one dealer consisted of 12,346 prints, 393 books, 351 copper plates, 88 lithographic stones and 33½ cwt. of letterpress. The supply of provincial centres was well organised, and a man who had recently died in prison, after a conviction obtained by the Society, had been in the habit of visiting the Universities of Oxford and Cambridge twice a year "with a stock of highly finished French prints far exceeding, if it be possible, the books that have been generally brought before the criminal courts."

This was enough for Campbell's case, but there were two other matters that he wished to mention. His reference to railway-bookstalls as distributors of *The Lady of the Camellias* had given pain to the Messrs W. H. Smith & Son, who held the contract for all the principal stations. He wished to say that he had a high opinion of the firm's respectability, a tribute which was at once capped by the Earl of Shaftesbury from a personal knowledge of these "truly Christian gentlemen." The publications in which they dealt, he rather ambiguously added, were as pure as those to be found in the most select library in the country.

It was Campbell's other apology for which the Lords were waiting. He had been informed, he now said, that on the second reading of the Bill he had been understood to make use of an expression of an insulting and offensive character to his noble and learned Friend opposite. If he had inadvertently let fall anything which might possibly be so construed, he begged most fully and entirely to retract it, and to express regret that he had said anything which might bear such a construction.

The moment had come for Lyndhurst's demonstration of how to accept an apology without really trying:

> I beg to acknowledge the full and proper manner in which my noble
> and learned Friend, the Lord Chief Justice, has atoned for what
> I considered to be most offensive words which he uttered with
> regard to myself on the second reading of this Bill. I did not hear
> the words myself, because I have the misfortune to labour under
> physical infirmity, but they were repeated to me by different friends,
> upon whose accuracy I most completely rely, and certainly they were
> of a most offensive nature. I apprehend, however, that my noble
> and learned Friend is not always aware of the effect of the expressions
> which he uses. He has been so accustomed to relate degrading anec-
> dotes of his predecessors in office, that I am afraid his feelings
> upon those subjects have become somewhat blunted.

In illustration of this condition Lyndhurst mentioned that he had been sent, with the author's compliments, the particular volume of Campbell's literary labours which contained paragraphs by no means complimentary to the recipient; and further, that after using in the House "expressions with regard to myself more degrading to the utterer than to the person against whom they were directed," the Chief Justice had come over to him with a smiling face and asked him to amend the Bill.

To amend, in the name of common sense, a measure "drawn in such a monstrous shape," Lyndhurst had sought to introduce safeguards against vexatious proceedings. As he now reminded the House, Tennyson's friend and publisher Moxon had some time ago been brought to court, with two other respectable booksellers, on a trumped up charge alleging blasphemy in a new edition of Shelley's poems. Having made his observations the old man left the Chamber, and the Bill skated through without further trouble.

"Our weather here is rising towards the intolerable point of heat," wrote Carlyle to his wife on 16 July. "Hotter today than ever, and next to no breath of wind going." He was spending these days as far as possible in the open, breakfasting under an awning in the garden and then working there, despite the abominated noises drifting over from the street, on the proofs of the first part of *Frederick the Great*. A little walk to Sloane Square to post his letters before five o'clock dinner, and his daily ride postponed till six on account of the heat. Then, if there were no visitors, more work till bed-time, when the sons and daughters of Belial would be streaming past on their way to the pleasures of Cremorne.

It was a profligate summer, a season bedizened and bedazzled. "We are overrun with royalties present and prospective," recorded Greville. "London is very gay," echoed Disraeli, reeling off a list of crowns and coronets and adding: "There is also a famous beauty here, the Comtesse Castiglione, who, as she is universally decried by all the grand ladies, I take it is of ravishing excellence." The Contessa was little more than sixteen, almost faultless in three or four languages, and of a classical beauty which Watts, from his vantage-point at Holland House where she was staying, was striving to convey in a painting which he did not have the chance to finish. As if all this were not enough to raise the eyebrows of her seniors, the child had two years before been consigned by her family to a loveless marriage in Italy and had then been deliberately exported, in furtherance of her country's political aspirations, to the French court. Her sensational triumph in Paris, including the inevitable appointment with Napoleon III in a shrubbery in the course of a *fête champêtre*, was now being followed, Disraeli presumed, by "a tour of conquest in foreign parts."

It was the Princess Royal's Prussian betrothal that conferred the inordinate glitter; and the Prussian Minister, Count Bernstorff, set competitors a cracking pace with the rout which he gave for the Queen and Court on 6 July. For Disraeli, who was there with his Mary Anne, "it recalled old days of Carlton House splendour, fanciful illuminations, and golden fish in endless fountains. There was a pavilion two hundred feet long, lined with the most splendid trees and shrubs I ever saw—araucarias and Norfolk Island pines." Three nights later there was a ball at Buckingham Palace. Next evening the Duchess of Manchester gave another, "of very *haut ton*," and the Queen had a concert. Moltke longed, or told his wife so, to get back to Germany, but his Prince's visit was extended to the fourteenth to take in the ceremony of the City's Freedom, after which the Prussian

Sensible Riding Costume for Warm Weather. From *Punch*, July, 1857

Hastings in Persistent Summer, October, 1857. Engraving after W. McConnell

Eastward Ho! August, 1857. By Henry Nelson O'Neil, A.R.A.

party left at last, but the Belgian, Dutch and other royalties remained.

The famous Holland House breakfasts (for which in fact people assembled at four in the afternoon and stayed till seven or eight) began on 15 July with seven hundred guests thronging the great reception-rooms, the conservatory, the gardens that had grown the first dahlias in England, the lawns terraced by William Kent. The Green Lane, bowered by trees and haunted by nightingales, led down to Little Holland House, where on Sunday afternoons pyramids of strawberries on long tables under the elms awaited the guests of the Prinseps. They played croquet or bowls, rubbed shoulders and dropped names, heard Joachim play, and Hallé, watched Miss Herbert, the actress-model, posing for young artists, talked poetry and philosophy, politics and fashion, and had almost ceased to wonder at unending summer. Up at the big house, where rain did fall on the morning of the twenty-fifth, Lady Holland was near to despair, for it was the day appointed for their fête. But by the afternoon the skies were clear and lovely again for the Queen of Holland, the Duchesse d'Orléans, the Duchesse d'Aumale, the Duchess of Cambridge, Princess May and some six hundred other guests.

The next day was Sunday, and in Chelsea Carlyle was still at his proofs: "slow like an old spavined horse, but never giving in; the gloom of my soul is perfect at times, for I have 'feverish headache' and *no* human company, or absolutely none that is not ugly to me." As always, the book was an oppression as well as an obsession, and often he dreamed of quitting London "for the sake of fresh air, and dairy-produce in abundance."

For his ride, however, it turned out to be "a genial, breezy summer evening, beautiful even in London." In Regent's Park he drew rein to watch, from a distance, the largest crowd he had seen in his life. Someone told him there were a hundred thousand gathered there, welcoming a sabbatarian breach of no little significance. For in the midst of them could be seen the upper part of a tent, and a streamer announcing "People's Band." The musicians had paused at that moment, and had they been playing Carlyle had no doubt that it would have been "vile opera trash." But the sight stirred him.

Men, women and children, all in their Sunday clothes, and quiet tho' lively, were moving, minutely, incessantly, far and wide, on their green floor under the sky: poor souls, after all! I found something respectable in this their success in getting a little wind-music for themselves, since all else was denied.

By contrast Hyde Park, when he rode back that way, seemed almost empty, for the Rotten Row cavalcade was over. But his route was crossed by "Dizzy and his old wife, taking an after-dinner drive; they looked content, 'peacefully sated with revenge and food,' and were not speaking one word."

Disraeli's mind, having fixed on the decision to challenge the Government next day on the subject of India, may have been occupied; for the speech when it came took three hours to deliver. Palmerston's mastery of compression, however, enabled him to report it to the Queen on the same evening in a dozen dismissive lines, with a summary of such critical observations as it provoked and a humorous touch for Mr Hadfield, the Member for Sheffield, who "shortly stated in his provincial dialect that 'we can never keep our 'old upon Hindia by the force of Harms.'" Among the ideas presented by Disraeli which the Prime Minister forebore to mention to Her Majesty were these:

> You ought at once, whether you receive news of success or defeat, to tell the people of India that the relation between them and their real Ruler and Sovereign, Queen Victoria, shall be drawn nearer. You must act on the opinion of India on that subject immediately; and you can only act upon the opinion of Eastern peoples through their imagination. You ought to have a Royal Commission sent by the Queen from this country to India immediately to inquire into the grievances of the various classes of that population. You ought to issue a Royal Proclamation to the people of India, declaring that the Queen of England is not a Sovereign who will countenance the violation of treaties; that the Queen of England is not a Sovereign who will disturb the settlement of property; that the Queen of England is a Sovereign who will respect their laws, their usages, their customs and, above all, their religion. Do this, and do it not in a corner, but in a mode and manner which will attract universal attention and excite the general hope of Hindostan, and you will do as much as all your fleets and armies can achieve.

It was the twenty-eighth day of the siege of the Lucknow Residency, and the first of the fantastic defence of the Little House at Arrah by a dozen or so civilians and fifty Sikh military police against a rebel force of several thousand with artillery. Sir Colin Campbell had impressed everybody by leaving London at a day's notice to take up the command in India, and Disraeli had now small prospect of an early escape to Torquay. With the temperature at eighty-six Palmerston had replied to a plea from Gladstone (whose eloquence, it was remarked, exuded from every pore) that he intended to keep the House at its labours as long as might be necessary. "I remember sitting in this House," he added, "until the middle of September."

England expected no less of her legislators now. The times were grave. The Divorce Bill must go through. Tearfully, as trouble gathered over the dear land of Shakespeare and of Dickens, and the family whose happiness it had been a privilege to share, Hans Andersen had torn himself away. For the room that he had occupied at Gad's Hill Place his host wrote out and affixed a memorial notice:

The great Danish writer Hans Andersen stayed in this room five weeks. And it seemed to the family five years.

A Hot Wind from Asia

Now all the youth of England is on fire. Now thrive the armourers, shaping for the short, square, vigorous person of William Morris a suit of mediaeval armour as complete as that of Sir Isumbras. The extravagance being delivered and donned, he complains that he can't bend his knees in it. But who, in 1857, wants to bend the knee? Come on, Topsy, read us one of your grinds:

> Swerve to the left, Son Roger, he said,
>   When you catch his eyes through the helmet-slit,
> Swerve to the left, then out at his head,
>   And the Lord God give you joy of it!

No news from Delhi, where the ten thousand British and Indians measure from the Ridge, under constant fire and sortie, in heat and sickness and indecision, the chances of assault upon walls held by thrice their number. But Dante Gabriel Rossetti, in an extraordinary release of animal spirits, is first up the scaling-ladder in the scaffolded Oxford Union, and the admiration of Burne-Jones has a new quality: "This man could lead armies and destroy empires if he liked!" The walls are new and unprepared, the tempera fails to hold, the practitioners are unskilled as to scale and technique. But the wombat is everywhere, multiplying on the whitewashed windows, scuttling in pen-sketches across Burne-Jones's despatches, drolly regardant on the imagined banner of the Jovial Campaign.

The offer of mural decorations for the Union—no fees, but expenses to be met—had been made in a burst of enthusiasm when Rossetti, who still lacked self-confidence in anything but water-colour, and Morris, who had scarcely painted at all, spent their torrid week-end in Oxford. Happily quartered now in the High, directly opposite Queen's, Rossetti, Morris and Burne-Jones were soon joined by Val Prinsep, the huge young son of the host and hostess of Little Holland House, who had had some lessons from Watts; Spencer Stanhope, also a Watts disciple; Arthur Hughes of the gorgeous *April Love*; and J. H. Pollen, Fine Art Professor at Dublin, the veteran of the company at forty and the only one with any experience of mural painting. Ford Madox Brown had been invited, but turned it down. So had Holman Hunt, but he too declined, thereafter exchanging with Millais some jealous reflections on Rossetti's almost effortless capture of the new young blood. The brilliant Pre-Raphaelite mirror had cracked. The web had floated wide. Knocking over their valuable cans of ultramarine, spilling things upon each other from great heights, consuming quantities of bottled soda-water sent over from The Star, scuffling and singing and cracking undergraduate jests like *O tempera, O Morris!*, the gay campaigners looked fearlessly down to Camelot.

Something must be set down to the Lady of Shalott herself, though she had made her first appearance in 1833. Still a favourite in 1857, she was portrayed twice, once by Rossetti and once by Hunt, in Moxon's new illustrated edition of Tennyson's poems. Hunt had taken a number of small liberties with the subject, and Tennyson expostulated: "I never said that the young woman's hair was flying all over the shop."

"No," Hunt composedly replied, "but you never said it wasn't." Rossetti caused the poet no misgivings with his own *Shalott* illustration: Sir Lancelot looking down by torchlight from the steps of the Camelot palace upon the dead face in the moored boat, that boat on which the lady's name had been written "underneath her stern" until Tennyson, warned of the invitation to unkind reviewers, altered it to "round the prow." But Gabriel was the last man to feel constrained by anything but his own imagination in illustrating someone else's poems; and his block for St Cecilia, chosen from *The Palace of Art*, struck most people as an enigma and some as an offence:

> Or in a clear-walled city on the sea,
>   Near gilded organ-pipes, her hair
> Wound with white roses, slept St. Cecily;
>   An angel looked at her . . .

Her eyes were closed, but she was not sleeping. Her hands on the key-board of the curious instrument, her body was arched back in ecstasy or orgasm within the sleeved embrace of the

angel who should have been simply looking at her: which
angel, in the words of the writer G. S. Layard, had become
"a great, voluptuous human being, not merely kissing (a sufficient incongruity in itself) but seemingly munching the fair face
of the lovely martyr." The whole picture, Layard concluded,
was "a subtle protest," "a sort of travesty"; the artist had drawn
"not an angel at all, but a man masquerading as an angel," an
all-too-earthly lover.

It might be so. The idealism in which Rossetti's aesthetic
imagination chose to luxuriate was kept in place by the worldly
candour with which he declared—and acted upon it—that women
were always nicer after they had lost their virginity. The dichotomy
of "soul at war with sense" that Tennyson read into the Arthurian
cycle could be accepted, but not the assurance of the victory
of soul; and Malory's version of the Matter of Britain, from which
Gabriel read aloud in his spell-binding voice to the already
converted Topsy and Ned, had a flavour that did not survive
the Laureate's promotion of King Arthur to the status of an
Eminent Victorian. Tennyson's Arthur might start by merging
with the dead Hallam and end by translation into the dead Prince
Consort. Rossetti, emerging from the emotional constrictions
of Chatham Place and *How They Met Themselves* to confront a
soaring, blank-arched wall in Oxford, re-imagined his own
divagations as he outlined the subject:

> Sir Lancelot prevented by his sin from entering the chapel of the
> San Graal. He has fallen asleep before the shrine full of angels, and
> between him and it, rises in his dream the image of Queen Guinevere,
> the cause of all. She stands gazing at him with her arms extended in
> the branches of an apple-tree.

The apple-tree, symbolic of the Fall, was as pervasive as the
wombat on the scribbled plaster; and Guinevere of course
began, though she was not to end, as the absent Lizzie. Morris
too had the adulterous queen in mind, and *The Defence of Guinevere* (no less) was to be the title of the poems he was assembling
for publication. Beneath the flowing draperies the Fleshly School
made its first faint signals. The worm was in the bud, the death-
watch beetle in the Table Round.

Consider, for instance, the risk that was being taken, before
the monarchy had been strengthened by the Camelot alliance,
in sending the young heir to the throne (albeit under strict

tutelage and the pseudonym of Baron Renfrew) on a Continental visit. Even the honour of providing a son as companion, which fell to Mr and Mrs Gladstone, was spotted with traces of apprehension. Writing to his wife on 28 July, just after consigning young Willy to those in charge of the trip, Gladstone had sought to allay her anxiety:

> I have sent Willy off to the Admiralty to dine and start. It may be no unimportant start for him, and unhappily it is one which has more risks of evil than likelihoods of good for an ordinary boy, but in his case we may, thank God, feel quite comfortable. The points of his character which will be tried by intercourse with the Prince are I think just those in which he is strongest . . .

The Prince was additionally fitted out with his father's private secretary, his father's equerry, two tutors, a naval doctor, and a load of precepts. Yet despite all this there came a summer evening at Königswinter when he was missed for a moment after supper and was presently apprehended in the act of kissing an attractive girl of about his own age. Willy Gladstone mentioned the rumpus in a letter to his mother, who informed her husband in London. Gladstone considered the matter, and wrote back:

> This little squalid debauch is, indeed, a paltry affair. But it makes one feel what we should, I think, have suspected—that the Prince of Wales has not been educated up to his position. This sort of unworthy little indulgence is the compensation. Kept in childhood beyond his time, he is allowed to make that childhood what it should never be in a Prince—or anyone else—namely, wanton.

The miniature royal turpitude fell tinkling on the pile of secret guilt, like the swords of the mortified officers whose sepoys had been disarmed at Peshawar. And still the sun shone on England, and there were times when even Carlyle could be charmed out of the strain and misery of his labour—as indeed he should have been when Jane wrote from Edinburgh, after he had sent her proof-sheets of the first two volumes: "Oh my dear! What a magnificent book this is going to be! The best of all your books. I say so, who never flatter, as you are too well aware . . ." On Sunday, 5 August, he started broad awake at three a.m., rose and went downstairs, and out into the dim, tranquil garden, where he sat on a stool and smoked—on an empty and treacherous stomach—a contemplative cigar.

Have not seen so lovely, sad and grand a summer for twenty years back. Trees stood all as if cast in bronze, not an aspen stirring; sky was a silver mirror, getting yellowish to the north-east, and only one big star, star of the morning, visible in the increasing light. This is a very grand place, this world, too. It did me no ill. Enough!

That evening a bank of cloud moved up the sky, and at night rainstorms spread over southern England, freshening town and country for another magnificent day. The Queen and her family were at Osborne in the Isle of Wight, where the sparkling morning brought Napoleon III and the Empress Eugénie up the Solent for a private visit in which, to the Queen's delight, the Government was counting on the Prince Consort's diplomatic gifts to strengthen the Anglo-French alliance. In Paris two years earlier she had been treated with much attention by the gallant Emperor ("the first man who had made love to her," said Lord Clarendon cattily), and on a return visit Eugénie had bequeathed the impression of a stately beauty and—to Mr Punch's almost weekly ridicule—the triumphant fashion of the crinoline. This she now re-imported, as Victoria recorded in a happy flurry of exclamation-marks, as formal evening wear, together with "charming but extremely simple" gowns for the day and a fixed habit of not coming down to breakfast.

"It was almost like a dream," wrote the Queen, and Albert concurred. The simplicity of it all was enchanting, the good nature, the delight of the visitors with every view and each flower-bed, their affectionate ways with the children, their bright interest in the improvements displayed for them on walks and drives through the estate. The Prince Consort paced the lawns in fatherly conversation with his well-mannered if not quite reliable guest, the archetype of the Frenchman of British caricature, short and spreading, with his imperial moustaches and beard, his conversational hands, his peg-top trousers. Eugénie captivated the Queen afresh with her womanly graces and her intellectual flair, and Napoleon intrigued her with accounts of "very strange things" effected by "Mr Hume" at his command séances in Paris.

There were some more showers during the visit, but the weather was superb when they re-embarked, and so continued. A week or so later, on a beautiful evening with the sea like oil, the *Victoria and Albert* took the royal family on a return trip to Cherbourg. A day was sufficient to satisfy the Prince's curiosity about the state of the Cherbourg defences, and they turned for home, where the latest intelligence from India apprised them that the rebels still held Delhi and that the good Sir Henry Lawrence had died from shell-wounds in the Lucknow Residency. The Queen felt obliged to repeat to Lord Palmerston that "the measures hitherto taken by the Government are not commensurate with the magnitude of the crisis."

The newspapers, and especially *The Times* under Delane, were by now giving the Indian situation the fullest coverage, printing the fortnightly despatches over several columns of blindingly small type, filling the intervals with all the private letters from the East that they could lay hands on, and supplementing their own magisterial comments with the controversial opinions of old India hands. There was much reflection on the obligations of Christian civilisation, and not a little on the nuisance of Christian missionaries. The unpublished opinion of Edward Fitz-Gerald, as a non-political orientalist, was that "a nation with great estates is like a man with them—more trouble than profit: I would only have a *competence* for my country as for myself." The measured conclusion of Charles Greville was that "Indians do not always know what is best for them, or most likely to promote their happiness, so it will not be surprising if these disorders should continue to increase, supposing the means of immediately and effectually suppressing them should be found wanting."

Awaiting in high expectation the triumph of the Atlantic Cable, the New York *Tribune* wished in the meantime to offer its readers some knowledgeable treatment by sea-mail of the events in India. It was thus that Karl Marx, fretting at the *Tribune*'s failure to do justice to the articles that he was supplying by arrangement, found himself suddenly, and with little equipment, in the position of a military correspondent. "The revolt in India," he had confessed to Engels on 19 July, "places me in some embarrassment." Engels had been working hard in Manchester on the composition of a military encyclopedia. Marx had helped by tracing some references at the British Museum, and could now turn confidently to his friend and benefactor:

If you can write a few general phrases for me it will be easy for me to make a readable article by using the material I have got together.

The situation of the rebels at Delhi and the movements of the English army are the only points on which, at the moment, I need a few military sentences.

He got his few sentences, but Engels was in a poor way of health, and getting worse. Marx peppered him with prescriptions, chiefly of cod-liver oil and iron, and urged the merits of the sea air at Hastings. Engels retreated instead to the Lancashire resort of New Brighton, and Marx soldiered on for the *Tribune* by his own wits. By 15 August he could tell Engels that "what I see in the Delhi affair is that the English will be obliged to retreat as soon as the rainy season sets in seriously." There must have been retired residents on the slopes of Hampstead who could have told him, had he been more sociable, that such few inches as an exhausted monsoon was likely to deposit upon Delhi had probably been welcomed already by the survivors of dust-storms and dehydration, heatstroke and flies and fevers. But his hypothesis, which he had boldly advanced on his own responsibility, seemed to him to speak for itself if previous reports could be relied upon. There might be awkward corners to turn as later news came in, "but with a little dialectic one will still get away with it. I have naturally given to my considerations such a form that in being wrong I shall still be right."

Through the August dog-days the Queen gave the Government no rest. Palmerston, on returning to Piccadilly after protracted sessions in the Commons, would find another memorandum, in a familiar hand, to be dealt with before he could retire. The royal minutes were formidable in their marshalling of military statistics and dispositions, but Cupid had had long practice in returning these darts, and he played the game with a distinct zest. When he gave an opening by reporting Parliamentary allegations of inadequate arrangements for home defence, meaning thereby to let the Queen understand that his hands were tied by votes on the estimates, Her Majesty came back with: "The Queen has just received Lord Palmerston's letter of yesterday, and must say that if she had been in the House she would have joined in saying that the Government were not doing enough to 'reorganise a defensive force for home service.' The Queen will write a memorandum on the subject . . . but in the meantime she must observe . . ." And so on, and so forth. But watch him save the point:

Viscount Palmerston presents his humble duty to your Majesty and has had the honour to receive your Majesty's communication of yesterday, stating what your Majesty would have said if your Majesty had been in the House of Commons. Viscount Palmerston may perhaps be permitted to take the liberty of saying that it is fortunate for those from whose opinions your Majesty differs that your Majesty is not in the House of Commons, for they would have had to encounter a formidable antagonist in argument, although on the other hand those whose opinions your Majesty approves would have had the support of a powerful ally in debate.

But with regard to the arrangements in connection with the state of affairs in India, Viscount Palmerston can assure your Majesty that the Government are taking, and will not fail to continue to take, every measure which may appear well adapted to the emergency, but measures are sometimes best calculated to succeed which follow each other step by step . . .

Had her Majesty been in a position to spend any part of this sweltering month in the House of Commons she might have found a sense of crisis overcoming bodily discomfort. Disraeli, having put forward his personal effort only to be charged with mischief-making, was keeping quiet. But Gladstone had conquered his fit of disgust with public affairs and come up from Cheshire by train, treating with cold silence a fellow-traveller's too-familiar offer of a nip of brandy and a fill of tobacco. "I never was engaged in any Parliamentary battle," he wrote to his wife, "in which I felt a deeper anxiety." And again: "All we can do is to put shoulder to shoulder and fight to the last. And this, please God, we will do."

Like Luther at Worms, like Lawrence at Lucknow, he could do no other. Clause by clause, and principle by principle, the Divorce Bill as sent down from the Lords must be fought "in the teeth of Lord Palmerston," and by methods which were generally regarded as setting a new precedent in technical obstruction as well as a new test of physical endurance. Objections and amendments from any part of the House, of which in so complex and tentative a measure there were necessarily many, were regularly extended by the eloquence of the Member for Oxford University, who thus stood forth in the Commons beside the Bishop of Oxford in the Lords, as the heroic champion of lost causes.

That the cause was in fact lost, that the Bill would be passed in this exhausting session unless the aged Prime Minister were struck down by apoplexy or the unpunctual comet, had been privately accepted by Gladstone when he set forth, in "mingled excitement and depression" to cleanse the vitiated air of public business. And the fervour of his hostility to the demoralising project of giving legal countenance to adultery, the passion of his rejection of a masculine privilege in infidelity, and the conviction of his observations in the field of lower-class morals, were all expended in the sole remaining hope of extricating the Church and the clergy from the operation of the fifty-third and last clause of the Bill. It was this clause which gave leave to the erring parties in a divorce to compound their adultery in the union of re-marriage. What several Bishops had been prepared to yield, Gladstone was religiously resolved to oppose. "The poor Church," he told his wife, "gets deeper and deeper in the mire."

Ten-hour sittings and two-hour speeches became almost commonplace. When he could get away between sittings, Gladstone would hurry over to his London base at 11, Carlton House Terrace, to take a bath and write a note to his wife; and to the Reform Club—where the great *chef* Alexis Soyer had touched nothing that he did not adorn—for a dish of his favourite mutton-chops. Outside Parliament he found other activities in the great cause for which six thousand clergy had been brought to sign a petition, but there was little time now for the nightly self-exposure of his rescue-work. And just outside his normal territory the harlot's cry from street to street was weaving old England's winding-sheet in the once respectable purlieus of Portlandia. The "Norton Street nuisance," which had roused the inhabitants of Portland Place to appeal to the Marylebone Vestry against scenes of nightly, and even daily, impropriety, was signalised in the *Saturday Review* as "the price which, in England, we pay for our social prudery": since it was unthinkable that the reforming measures presented to Parliament would ever go to the length of controlling prostitution by legalising it.

Sandwiched between solemn articles on India, and learned reviews of the first volume of Buckle's monumental *History of Civilization in England*, the periodicals that followed each other, crisp and fresh, on the polished table-tops of the Pall Mall clubs, treated with a specious show of reluctance the evidence of social iniquities. Nothing pointed more dramatically to a canker at the heart of things than the abandonment at this moment of the annual cricket-matches at Lord's between Eton and Harrow and other leading Public Schools. Though received with under-standable dismay, this breach with tradition—happily temporary—was justified by the charge that the matches "brought together a number of boys who practically had the run of the metropolis for a week, unchecked by any control, and that they were led by bad example into the debauchery for which London offers such glaring facilities."

But the case which found even the *Saturday Review* straining for a metaphor ("the bladder must swell to all but impossible dimensions before it bursts") provided support for the Divorce Bill, and especially for Lyndhurst's efforts in the Upper House, as the criminal conversation trial to end them all. The action of a Charlotte Street upholsterer called Lyle against his partner called Herbert, which was heard during August, was in fact the last of the crim-con cases. As such it was distinguished not only by the patent element of conspiracy but by the first and only intro-duction of an ingenious device for measuring the incidence of adultery by means of a clockwork attachment to the bedsprings. Having more or less thrown his wife at his business associate, Mr Lyle employed the inventor of the crim-con-meter, by name Taylor, for a fee of £20, and on a given night the contraption was wired through to the bedroom from a room rented in the next house. The arrangements were so complete that the cheerfully injured husband could watch directly through a hole pierced in the wall, as well as indirectly by means of the indicator, and could finally gain access through the roof and a trap-door to accost the bed's occupants. He then celebrated his success, on gin and pickled salmon, with the inventor and some invited friends. The subsequent descriptions in court of the workings of the crim-con-meter caused roars of laughter, but the whole entertainment was derisorily rewarded by damages of one farthing.

It was not only the baleful countenance of divorce that kept Members of Parliament at their post in the summer of peril. The Bill for more effectually preventing the Sale of Obscene Books, Pictures, Prints and other Articles had also descended to the Commons, and with it Lord Campbell in person, to watch its progress from the gallery in a manner which stung the Speaker to complain afterwards of an attempt to overawe them.

They could at least ask pointed questions as to why Scotland should be excluded from the Bill's effect. They could give another little run to the idea that some passages from Lord Campbell's own literary output might be made the subject of prosecutions if his Bill became law. They could add to Lyndhurst's examples of actionable classics the *Basia* of Johannes Secundus, the works of Aristophanes and Martial, and of Pope (containing "passages which no decent woman could say she had read"). They could find in the House of Commons Library a set of illustrated volumes on the antiquities of Pompeii which had already been condemned to destruction in America under a law such as was now proposed for England. They could warn of the dangers of giving special powers to magistrates. What they could no more do, in this House than in the other, was to expose themselves by dissenting from the purpose of a measure that many of them disliked. It was Richard Monckton Milnes, suitably enough, who came nearest to the heart of things, opposing the Bill as "totally alien to the habits of this country; certain, in the end, to be disgustful to the English people; and one which would never have reached its present shape if Hon. Members had had the manliness to state what were their real views on the subject."

Monckton Milnes had won the undergraduate admiration of Swinburne as the first and covertly recognised authority on the Marquis de Sade; but the fine copies of *Justine* and the rest formed only one section of the extensive *enfer* which itself was but one department of the library at Fryston Hall. Reasonably alarmed by the powers of entry, seizure and arrest sought to be given to the law, Milnes showed equal concern in Parliament to protect the well-established booksellers whose large stocks might so easily contain (as he knew because he patronised them) the occasional choice item. "The evil complained of," he assured the House, was "limited to two or three streets in the Metropolis." The products of Holywell Street that had shaken the Chief Justice were indeed a world away from the bibliophile's treasures on which Milnes would leave his week-end guests to browse on Sunday mornings while, like a good landowner, he worshipped with his lady and his tenants. Considering the superb editions of Restif de la Bretonne and de Nerciat, Diderot and Mirabeau, all with their special engravings, the illustrated French translation of *Fanny Hill*, the *Sonnetti Lusuriosi* of Aretino with its famous positional plates, and the many other gems of his library, it has occurred to many to speculate with a certain awe on the consequences of bringing home Florence Nightingale, as Milnes had come fairly near to doing, as *châtelaine* of Fryston. But the charming Annabel Crewe, after all, either didn't know or didn't care about the contents of her husband's particular cases; and by now Milnes had grown podgy, while Miss Nightingale had just been told that her life was not worth twenty-four hours' purchase – a verdict with which she almost exultingly agreed.

The four-month operations of the Royal Commission on the Health of the Army which Florence had forced upon the stone-walling Panmure had been carried with her own unmatchable concluding evidence, to an acceptance on which she marginally noted that "Reports are not self-executive." The much larger volume of her own *Notes on Matters affecting the Health, Efficiency and Hospital Administration of the British Army*, poured out at the same time and at incredible speed, was still in manuscript. Both told, with facts, figures, tables and detailed testimony, a story which might have put heart into those challengers in distant lands on whose impudence Palmerston had ridden back to power. Although the Crimean horrors could be seen as a test-case of what could be and had been overcome by resolute remedies, and although the expeditionary force for China, now partly diverted to India, had not been allowed to leave until Miss Nightingale had had her say, the normal peace-time mortality in the barracks of the British Army was now unanswerably shown to be at least double that of the none-too-pampered civilian population subsisting outside of them. "Our soldiers," said Miss Nightingale, "enlist to death in the barracks."

It seemed that the same might be said of the Commander-in-Chief (as Sidney Herbert called her) when she took up her campaign headquarters in the Burlington Hotel. Her mother and her sister Parthenope had to live with her in order that she should continue her great work. So, at least, they had convinced them-selves, but in her own later recollection their sole occupation, apart from some involvement with the London season, had been "to lie on two sofas and tell one another not to get tired by putting flowers into water." The summer heat that beat upon the ill-ventilated and ill-lit rooms turned in August to a humid oppression under skies that were often leaden and over-cast. Succumbing by inches to intolerable fatigue, living for weeks on nothing whatever but tea, she attained the immediate goal of her endeavours and on 11 August, promptly and inevitably, collapsed. But at Malvern, whither she escaped—blessedly alone—to take a cure, she continued to work in a wildly obsessive way. Harriet Martineau, another formidable woman who influenced London opinion by remote control from the Lake District, wrote her obituary and had it set in type. Miss Nightingale was thirty-seven, and hell-bent on sacrificing her life if it should take another half-century. Which it did.

It was Sidney Herbert whose symptoms of exhaustion—the "fancies" rebuked by his beloved taskmistress—were those of mortal disease. The campaign, however, had been brought to a point where he could get away to Ireland for the fishing. Lord Panmure, their battered adversary, felt he had earned his recreation among the grouse-butts, but was officially recalled from Scotland just before the magic Twelfth. And Parliament was still tethered. In the Commons the moral thunder growled over now snoring back-benchers, and even the least sensitive suffered a new visitation of summer. This invaded the Chamber with the same perceptible stench that had risen to Miss Nightingale's nostrils when the water-carts went by in Piccadilly on their supposedly merciful errand. On 28 July there had been a complaint that "some of the officers of the House were so affected in their health by the effluvia of the Thames that it was difficult for them to perform their duties." The Members blamed the First Commissioner of Works, or alternatively the Metropolitan Board. Some blamed the creeping approach of noisome factories, others the odour of sanctity or the reek of adultery. An outspoken few took exception when the Queen, leaving them in session, went north to Balmoral. And *Punch* adapted Hood's *Song of the Shirt* to the ordeal of Westminster:

> Talk! Talk! Talk!
> In the blazing midsummer light;
> Talk! Talk! Talk!
> Through the sweltering midsummer night:
> While all about the House
> The bone-boilers' odours cling,
> To mock us with dreams of the heathery hills,
> Where the grouse are on the wing.

Yet they held out, as their countrymen in Lucknow, in conditions

Alfred Tennyson photographed by Lewis Carroll (Dodgson) at Tent Lodge, Coniston, September, 1857

The Dancing-Platform at Cremorne. By Phoebus Levin

The Fairy-Feller's Masterstroke (detail). By Richard Dadd

The Patent Crim-Con Meter. From *Paul Pry*, November, 1857

which the Poet Laureate must finally immortalise, were even then
holding out.

> Heat like the mouth of hell, or a deluge of cataract skies,
> Stench of old offal decaying, and infinite torment of flies.

Relief came at last, with the Prorogation on 28 August by
Commission, the Royal Assent to the Divorce and Matrimonial
Causes Bill, and the reading by the Lord Chancellor of the
Queen's speech. Her Majesty "would omit no Measure calculated
to quell the grave Disorders in *India*, and was confident that,
with the Blessing of Providence, the powerful means at Her
Disposal would enable Her to accomplish that task." Both
Houses were thanked for making provision for the Princess
Royal on her approaching marriage, and for passing with zeal
and assiduity the Divorce and other important Acts. The Obscene Publications (Prevention) Act, which was to govern the
matter for a century, nestled anonymously among those "further
Acts of less Importance which had met with Her Majesty's
ready consent."

And now for the wholesome air of a lovely countryside,
for fields more abundant in harvest than most men could remember, for rivers richly stocked and moors where birds of a torpid
plumpness awaited their delayed decimation. For unarmed
holidays the English Lake District was much favoured. Alpine
travel, powerfully publicised according to their respective lights
by John Ruskin and Albert Smith, had become so popular that
The Times complained of increasing boredom with ascents of
Mont Blanc. Huxley and Tyndall made for Switzerland with
their knapsacks and geological hammers and collecting-boxes.
Macaulay, on the eve of a sedate Continental excursion, marked
28 August as a great day in his life, even though most of it
was spent at home, "very sad about India."

> I went, very low, to dinner, and had hardly begun to eat when a
> messenger came with a letter from Palmerston. An offer of a peerage;
> the Queen's pleasure already taken. I was very much surprised . . .
> I had no hesitation about accepting, with many respectful and grate-
> ful expressions; but God knows that the poor women at Delhi
> and Cawnpore are more in my thoughts than my coronet.

Shaftesbury too, taking the waters at Spa, "in capital walking trim and a good appetite," could not shake off India, and devoted himself on 29 August to recording the "number and variety of things to be prayed for."

> That He will quell the mutiny and give us a speedy victory; that He will make this outbreak the commencement of a new order of things; of a wiser and more vigorous government; of justice and judgment; of greater knowledge and greater zeal for man's real good; of fresh openings for the advance of the Gospel; of enlarged missionary operations; of increased opportunity to promote and invite the Second Advent.
>
> That He will protect, shelter, and deliver from their unspeakably ferocious enemies, the helpless women and children outraged, tortured, murdered by the incarnate fiends of Hindostan . . .

He also had an idea, about which he at once wrote to Palmerston, Panmure and others, for raising reinforcements from Africa.

> The Africans are eager for employment, they make first-rate soldiers, would bear the Indian climate, and have no fraternisation with the natives. Cheaper, too, by far. Ardently do I pray that this plan may be adopted. What a lift also to the nigger! and what a blow to the slave-trade!

X

AUGUST–SEPTEMBER
Various Vacations

A SUMMER IN which Manchester was starred for tourists could be called historic. For Mrs Gaskell, who happened to live there with her husband, it became a matter of bracing herself for yet another week of coping with enthusiastic house-guests. When a stranger enquired with a rapt look if that were *the* Miss Nightingale whom she was conducting round the Art Treasures Exhibition, she had not the heart to deny him his innocent satisfaction. But of course it was Parthenope who was there with her mother; and when the story got about it was unkindly taken to reflect upon the regard for truth of an authoress who had already been in trouble over her Brontë book.

The cloaked and bearded vision of the Poet Laureate, however, was unmistakable when he visited the Exhibition at the end of July. When a local magnate introduced himself with the offer of an evening's hospitality at his suburban seat, Tennyson gruffly countered with "What shall we do there?" But he accepted on further pressure, and though the company bewildered him he stayed into the small hours. Nathaniel Hawthorne, who frequented the great pavilion at Old Trafford over many weeks, was equally pleased to have the poet pointed out to him. But his reaction was more delicate:

> Gazing at him with all my eyes, I liked him well, and rejoiced more in him than in all the other wonders of the Exhibition . . . I would most gladly have seen more of this one poet of our day, but forbore to follow him; for I must own that it seemed mean to be dogging him through the saloons, or even to look at him, since it was to be done stealthily, if at all.

The American included in his studies of the Exhibition the refreshment rooms, where "John Bull and his wife may be seen in full gulp and guzzle, swallowing vast quantities of cold boiled beef, thoroughly moistened with porter or bitter ale:

and very good meat and drink it is." A regulation against the introduction by visitors of their own food and drink, however, put the attendants to considerable trouble by the smuggling in of bread-and-cheese in top hats and of brandy in quinine-bottles.

Was it all a success? The guarantors had a deficit of £1,000 to meet when the great show closed its doors at the end of October, but it had been a pioneering undertaking. Hallé was persuaded by it that the northern city was the place to bring his orchestra into being. In the business world the wide interest that had been generated could be gauged by the advertisement of oil-paintings, conveniently small, warranted genuine by the factory and exported to America at six shillings and ninepence apiece. This item seems to have escaped the notice of Ruskin, who had made his main visit in July, when he delivered at the Manchester Athenaeum the two lectures subsequently famous as *The Political Economy of Art*. Any of the assembled worthies who had been expecting his congratulations must have been crestfallen as they struggled to digest his withering sermons on the proper application of wealth to social improvement, and on artistic genius as an economic factor.

The ennobling arts had their slow way to make. For the release of a dithyrambic frenzy two nights in the Free Trade Hall had been enough. That Dickens "literally electrified the audience" with his Manchester performances of *The Frozen Deep* on 21 and 22 August was for once, Wilkie Collins alarmingly recorded, "a statement of fact." As for the effect on Dickens himself, he had become, as he told a friend, "the modern embodiment of the old Enchanters, whose Familiars tore them to pieces. I weary of rest, and have no satisfaction but in fatigue." Hans Andersen had tiptoed from the scene, leaving the world's supplier of breathingly realistic toys the self-confessed victim of a faery thrall:

> I wish I had been born in the days of Ogres and Dragon-guarded Castles. I wish an Ogre with seven heads (and no particular evidence of brains in the whole of them) had taken the Princess whom I adore—you have no idea how intensely I love her!—to his stronghold on the top of a high series of mountains, and there tied her by the hair. Nothing would suit me half so well this day, as climbing after her, sword in hand, and either winning her or being killed. *There's* a frame of mind for you, in 1857.

So intimate a disclosure could not be made—or at all events not yet—to Angela Burdett-Coutts. But just in case that lady had been prompted by some wind of rumour to identify a princess in the story, Dickens sent her, after returning to Gad's Hill, a charming account of the impression made upon him in Manchester by "the womanly tenderness of a very good little girl who acted Mary's part." The role involved, among other telling moments, the unforgettable climax which Dickens made of the dying Wardour, over whom as the good little girl knelt in farewell "the tears streamed out of her eyes into his mouth, down his beard, all over his rags—down his arms as he held her by the hair." It had been in vain for Dickens to whisper between his lines "My dear child, it will be over in two minutes." By the time the curtain fell she had set half the cast, to say nothing of the audience, crying with her. It was all so prettily simple and unaffected. "And if you ever see, at Kean's or elsewhere, Miss Maria Ternan, that is the young lady."

Yet we all know, in our horrible posthumous way, that it was not Maria Ternan who had caught Charles Dickens at the vulnerable climactic of forty-five. It was her fair-haired, blue-eyed eighteen-year-old sister Ellen, who even before the Manchester crisis had compensated a slightly less prominent part in the play with an invasion of the Dickens heart and household. Some kind of fate, if not some kind of comet, had brought Mrs Ternan and her daughters to this particular theatrical appointment at the moment when their famous employer's sense of the might-have-been was rising up to choke him. He had not, until this wombat-haunted year, been the sort of man, or the sort of writer, to sacrifice a widely respected domesticity on the promptings of suppressed disharmony. The suggestions of a separation that had broken once or twice upon the rock of the various proprieties had come from his wife, not from himself. Certainly it was foolish of him, when his professional recruits were rehearsing during the London performances for the Jerrold Fund, to order from a jeweller a real bracelet as a present for Ellen in her part in the farce of Uncle John. It was unfortunate that the parcel was mistakenly delivered to Mrs Dickens. It was unkind of him to meet this situation by insisting, in the face of his wife's tears, that she should make a social call upon her girlish rival. But she dried her eyes and went. And there's a frame of mind for you, in 1857.

In a trough of "low pulse, low voice, low spirits" after the manic experience in Manchester, Dickens selected for escape the frowning fells of Cumberland, and Collins as the companion who could best help him to forget that he was the father of ten. Climbing a mountain on the second day out, Collins sprained his ankle, and the father of ten had to carry him back to their inn, and in and out of railway-carriages as they moved on. Dimly reflected for the readers of *Household Words*, the expedition became *The Lazy Tour of Two Idle Apprentices*.

The title would have better fitted the Scottish jaunt which Lewis Carroll was making with his schoolmaster contemporary Barclay. A morning mist was enough to deter them from the ascent of Ben Lomond, but they did some sightseeing by coach and loch-steamer and rail, and some theatre-going in Edinburgh and Glasgow. A version of *Faust* which drew wild applause from a Glasgow gallery was allowed by Dodgson to be both beautiful and cleverly acted, but it was strong meat for his delicate constitution. His blood ran cold at the spectacle of Marguerite writhing like a fascinated animal and uttering low, despairing shrieks as Mephistopheles gloated upon her agony. At last came the descent of Mephisto and Faust into a trap-door hell, with Marguerite floating up to the welcoming angels, and this struck him as profane—nearly as bad, indeed, as the way that the Greeks made sport of their religion and their gods.

> I don't think this ultra-realising of things to us (at present) abstractions, can tend to good: it must lean far more to infidelity . . . I think it is a play that should never have been put on the stage—it is too horrible, and too daring in its representation of the spirit-world.

Happily for Lewis Carroll, composure could be recovered in the Scottish National Gallery, where in Sir Joseph Noel Paton's picture of *Oberon and Titania* he counted as many as a hundred and sixty-five fairies, a representation of the spirit-world that was beyond impeachment. It was a time when the population-explosion in Fairyland gave full employment to artists as charmingly laborious as Paton, as exquisitely disturbed as Dadd, as prolific in talent as Richard Doyle, whose studio was so crowded with his tiny ectoplasmic sitters that he could slip a priapic Lord of Misrule into the familiar cover of *Punch* without noticeable offence. Even when the possibilities of Oberon's special kingdom seemed to have been exhausted, Christina Rossetti would have new sports and species with which to confuse natural selection in her market of goblins:

> One had a cat's face,
> One whisked a tail,
> One tramped at a rat's pace,
> One crawled like a snail,
> One like a wombat prowled obtuse and furry . . .

Scotland had soothed John Ruskin also. The relentless devotion of his parents, with whom he had been in Highland retreat for the past couple of months, could not sour the pleasures of a summer so wonderfully fine that it scarcely seemed the same landscape as that sodden setting in which the triangle of forces had rearranged itself to dispose of his unfortunate marriage. So smiling was the harvest of oats as he moved about that for once he could asperse the vine-lands that had given his father and himself so many travel-memories, and the means of so comfortable an income. The fields of Scotland's staple crop seemed prettier now than any vintage; "for a vintage," he wrote to his American friend Norton, "is a great mess." The squeezing of grapes, Ruskin had suddenly decided, was after all a pity—"much more when it comes to dancing among the grapes with bare feet, and other such arcana of Bacchanalian craft." Not only was the sickle a more comely instrument than any that he had seen employed in viticulture. It was also, he felt, more serviceable in metaphor.

Just south of the Border in Northumberland, the well-placed Wallington estate secured for the hospitable Lady Trevelyan the chance of introducing Ruskin to young Swinburne, who had himself been scrambling about the highlands and islands. At the same pregnant moment Lewis Carroll, having now conveyed himself to Ambleside in Lakeland, was stalking with his photographic equipment the majestic quarry of Tennyson. From his pocketful of metaphorical white stones one could be impulsively assigned to Friday, 8 September, when he made his way to the head of Coniston Water to present himself at Tent Lodge, the retreat that had been lent to the Tennysons by an open-handed citizen of Leeds. The Laureate had stumped off by himself for the day, but Dodgson was graciously received by Mrs Tennyson and given an appointment for the following day, by which time he had moved to the Coniston hotel and was back on the doorstep at noon.

Tennyson must have expected that his visitor, however diffident, would have textual enquiries to make. Visitors nearly always did. One lady had presumed that the birds in the high Hall garden who called "Maud!" were nightingales, and had to be sharply told that they were rooks. The poet had some concern for accuracy, was disturbed at having supposed, on a very early experience of the railway in 1830, that the wheels ran in grooves and—returning to ornithology—endured from Canon Rawnsley a long inquisition set going by the "sea-blue bird of March" in *In Memoriam*. Tennyson himself thought he had had the kingfisher in mind, and had answered other enquirers in that sense. But the Canon argued until, with a sigh, the Poet gave in: "Well, well, make it a tit." Now there was a young mathematical tutor to deal with, asking him to explain passages that he had imagined to be perfectly clear. Having disposed of one of them, in *Maud*, he was requested to elucidate the lines:

> Dowered with the hate of hate, the scorn of scorn,
> The love of love . . .

Any meaning that the words might fairly bear, he affably replied, would be acceptable to him, but the construction that he recollected was "hatred of the quality of hate, and so on." Pressed to agree that it could also mean "the *quintessence* of hate, of scorn, of love," he indulgently allowed his caller to carry away the impression that that would be finer.

As a Lewis Carroll day it was really wonderful, on through lunch at one house, dinner at another, fun with the photograph album and memorably contemptuous remarks about Ruskin. It went on so late that he had to wait at his hotel door, ringing the bell, until someone got up to let him in. This was all beyond white stones. This was set down as *Dies mirabilis*.

Havelock's Highlanders on that day reached the outskirts of Lucknow. Delhi had been retaken by storm a week earlier. But in Balmoral Castle, where this could not be known, a small quorum of the Privy Council was gathering, summoned from their country seats to order in the Queen's name a national Day of Prayer and Humiliation. It was Palmerston, quaintly enough, who had proposed this recourse in what he called for the first time "the present calamitous state of affairs in India." The Queen herself considered that the last such occasion during the Crimean War had done more harm than good. She would have preferred a day of "intercession for our suffering countrymen," and to have it appointed for a Sunday, when it stood some chance of being generally observed. But Palmerston, though he had no intention of himself going all the way to Scotland for a Council, wanted humiliation and wanted it on a weekday. So far as the Royal Proclamation could be effective, he got both, fixed for Wednesday, 7 October.

Balmoral was a place that braced the Queen physically and relaxed her mentally. It exercised the Prince's restless talents for estate development as well as his proper pride in the acquisition of antlered heads, and it wrapped them both in the feudal fairy-tale of a forest-lordship. To this the local inhabitants, independent but respectful, lent themselves with unselfconscious ease, and the discreet establishment of comfort-stations within walking- and riding-distance of the Castle enabled the fantasy to be indulged with assurance. "The place and environs are pretty," noted Charles Greville, summoned from London as Clerk to the Privy Council, and the rooms in the Castle few, small, but not uncomfortable. It was his first visit, and his notions of a rural *pièd-à-terre* had been formed as an occasional guest at Chatsworth and Blenheim.

This year, however, the autumnal picture had a poignant tinge as the young Princess Royal accepted in humble shielings a neighbourly farewell. Hour by hour she was approaching the state which had been presented to her as combining all the elements of earthly bliss with those of an indescribable ordeal. Her father and mother had by now ceased to blame each other for the dynastic sacrifice of their scarcely fledged firstborn. They could remind themselves that it was here, at the bend of a moun-tain-path for ever sacred, that true affection had descended two years ago when Vicky and her Fritz had been allowed to lag behind the rest of the party. But Vicky was still the apple of her father's eye, and separation drew nearer with each period of the daily instruction that he was giving her in her future duties; while her mother noted wanly of every family pleasure that it would not, in a united sense, occur again. The Princess was a cheerful and sensible girl, but in all the circumstances her stomach-upsets were not surprising.

Nor was Scotland, whose nationals from field-officer to ranker were prominently engaged in the Indian troubles, a place in which the hot winds of horror could be forgotten. In letters to her foreign relatives the Queen pointed out how different it all was from the Crimean affair, where the ladies and children were not in danger and where one was dealing with a declared national enemy, not with "our own people whom we had trusted." She further explained that the casualties this time were more widely felt:

> There is hardly a family who has not either lost a relation or is not in anxiety about them. This is more amongst the gentry and middle classes than in the very highest circles, there are few of those as yet. Some poor people have three sons in India, either in the Military or Civil Service, and all equally exposed to be killed.

The class-aspect of things had also fascinated the editor of the *Saturday Review*. At the end of the first week in August, when the sense of atrocity had begun to harden with the news of the river-massacre at Cawnpore of 27 June, a leading article declared:

> There are seasons in which the thirst for revenge and the purpose of chastisement blend with each other, and become indistinguishable. This is one of those seasons, and it will go ill with any Government which tries to baulk the nation of its desire.

Such was "the steadfast mind," it was claimed, "of the middle sections of society" which monopolised the *de facto* government of India by services "extensively recruited from the all-powerful class which lies between the outskirts of the peerage and the frontier-line of the shopkeepers."

This being a fair description of the readership of *Punch*, no quarter for "sepoy-lovers" was to be expected in its weekly repertory. Puns almost as excruciating as the topics that inspired them were presently followed by cartoons in which a charging lion interrupted the activities of a man-eating tiger, and smocked English yokels forsook the festival of harvest-home at the call of distant service. The private comments of literary men were even more eloquent of shocked sensibilities than the drumming of the larger part of the Press. Carlyle drew a simple moral:

> Tongue cannot speak the horrors that were done on the English

by those mutinous hyaenas. Allow hyaenas to mutiny and strange things will follow.

Kingsley was racked in his own person by vicarious torment:

> I can think of nothing but these Indian massacres. The moral problems they involve make me half mad. Night and day the heaven seems black to me, though I was never so prosperous and blest in my life as now. I can hardly bear to look at a woman or a child— even at my own beloved ones sometimes. It raises such horrible images from which I can't escape. What does it all mean? Christ is King nevertheless. I tell my people so . . .
>
> Only by going into hell can one rise again the third day. I have been in hell many times in my life . . . but I have never looked hell so close in the face as I have been doing of late.

Dickens exposed to Angela Burdett-Coutts a stark reaction which perhaps served as cover for the domestic rebellion which he could not yet admit to her:

> And I wish I were Commander-in-Chief in India. The first thing I would do to strike that Oriental race with amazement . . . should be to proclaim to them, in their language, that I considered my holding that appointment, by the leave of God, to mean that I should do my utmost to exterminate the Race upon whom the stain of the late cruelties rested; and that I begged them to do me the favour to observe that I was there for that purpose and no other, and was now proceeding, with all convenient dispatch and merciful swiftness of execution, to blot it out of mankind and raze it off the face of the earth.
>
> My love to Mrs Brown . . .

These sampled sentiments were all set down after the shudder of the second Cawnpore outrage—the slaughter of the women and children—had travelled from its epicentre to reach England in the first golden days of September. Such details as the refusal of Nana Sahib's sepoys to carry out the obscenity were not revealed until months later, and then largely disregarded. But the inescapable evidence of the bloodstained room and the choked well conferred verisimilitude on all the horror-stories that had been circulating since July, when Monckton Milnes had regaled his Mayfair breakfast-parties with red-hot items from his

private mail from India. Whether he believed all that his corres-
pondents told him is not easy to determine, but the sex-'n'-
violence section of his library was now augmented by the
commonplace-book in which he was recording episodes of an
appropriate kind, blindings and castrations and burnings-alive,
horrid rapes before the parents' eyes, husbands bound to trees
to witness enormities upon their wives.

It was as if the actual killings were not enough, the sudden
treacheries, the fierce assaults on the defenceless, the destruction
of witnesses by men who knew that they had themselves no
mercy to expect. And perhaps they were not enough. Something
in the situation demanded the sexual tribute to racial excitement
which the mutineers at their most savage were curiously dis-
inclined to pay. The innumerable accounts of rape and mutilation
were never substantiated. Only one abduction, of an Eurasian
girl who took no great harm from it, was eventually proved.
But the ascertainable facts of history are not always enough for
its emotions—as none knew better than Carlyle, the kindler of
furious prose-poetry from the eleutheromaniac destruction of
a Bastille containing seven unimportant prisoners.

Disraeli was not alone in maintaining reservations about the
Indian catastrophe, but he was the one most publicly committed.
In Parliament at the end of July he had offered two main proposi-
tions. One had been that "the rise and fall of empires are not
affairs of greased cartridges. Such results are occasioned by
adequate causes and by an accumulation of adequate causes."
In suggesting, without at the time much evidence, that events
had the aspect of rebellion rather than mutiny, he had widened
the subject to indict administrations in India and in Britain, past
and present, for misjudged policies and a general failure to
appreciate Oriental viewpoints. His second proposition followed
logically enough: that, although "a merely military mutiny may
be met by a merely military effort," the profound problems that
would remain in this case demanded immediate attention to a
hearts-and-minds campaign. Of this the minimum principle was
that "we ought to temper justice with mercy—justice the most
severe with mercy the most indulgent."

Neither of these ideas was neglected by the newspapers, and
the controversy raged with especial bitterness between those
who blamed the outbreak upon too much Christian interference
and those who saw it as a judgement on too little. But the Palmer-

ston Government, which had shown that barbarian savagery was a dependable asset in face of Disraeli's earlier challenge on China, had little to fear now from an aroused Press. With *The Times* in full thunder, and "justice with mercy" a favourite text for leading articles, the scales were tipped at an increasing angle. In Shaftesbury's final and public formulation, though revenge must be banished from thoughts and lips, "the retribution that follows upon these crimes must be equal to the nature and extent of the crimes themselves."

In the meantime Disraeli confined his vein of sarcasm to private communications. "It is only for your own ear," he cautioned Lady Londonderry on 16 September, when expressing his suspicion "that many of the details of horrors, which have so outraged the sensibility of the country, are manufactured." Even the heroic story of an officer saving—and using—the last bullet for his wife, which must have gratified more sensibilities than it outraged, appeared now to have been an interpolation. The poem that the supposed incident had drawn from Christina Rossetti (*In the Round Tower at Jhansi*) was rated among her masterpieces by her brother William Michael, and a touch of Disraeli's own professional admiration could be spared for the myth's originator: "It was no rude hand that forged this tale of plaintive horror," and those who put it about were plainly capable of other fictions:

> Details are a feature of the Myth. The accounts are too graphic—
> I hate the word. Who can have seen these things? Who heard them?
> ... Who that would tell these things could have escaped?

He was not really trying to prove a negative, but he suspected, among other things, Palmerston's notorious skill in manipulating the Press. "The passions of the people are diverted thus from misconduct of their Government."

Spending the recess in the peaceful comfort of Hughenden Manor, Disraeli could even affect to be somewhat out of touch with the latest news or pseudo-news. At the end of September, however, for the first time in two months, he let himself go at a Farmers' Dinner at Newport Pagnell:

> The horrors of war need no stimulant. The horrors of a war carried
> on as the war in India is at present especially need no stimulant. I
> am persuaded that our soldiers and our sailors will exact a retribution

which it may perhaps be too terrible to pause upon. But I do
without the slightest hesitation declare my humble disapproba-
tion of persons in high authority announcing that upon the standard of England "vengeance" and not "justice" should be inscribed
. . . I, for one, protest against taking Nana Sahib as a model for the
conduct of the British soldier.

The Nana Sahib's animus, so long concealed and so horribly
satisfied, stemmed from the discontinuance of the pension he
had been receiving as the son of a conquered house. Living
in England at this time was another dispossessed Prince, the
nineteen-year-old Maharaja Duleep Singh. He was the youngest son
of the great Sikh ruler Ranjit Singh, an ally of the British for
thirty years; and when the Punjab was annexed after the Sikh
Wars that followed Ranjit's death, the boy Maharaja had been
given a pension and the formal right to keep his title, in exchange
for loyalty to the British power. He became a Christian, "the
first of his high rank who has embraced our faith," as Victoria
remarked with approval. He further delighted her, when he came
to England, by his pleasant manners and good looks.

At this juncture it occurred to somebody that a public denun-
ciation by Duleep Singh of the rebel excesses would have an
excellent effect – though on whom is not very clear, since the
British were already receiving surprisingly staunch assistance
from the Sikhs. The young man demurred, and Clarendon wrote
to the Queen to suggest that she might add her persuasion. From
Balmoral on 23 September the Queen sent back a piece of her
mind:

> Though we might perhaps have wished the Maharajah to express
> his feelings on the subject of the late atrocities in India, it was hardly
> to be expected that he . . . should pronounce an opinion on so painful
> a subject, attached as he is to his country, and naturally *still* posses-
> sing, with all his amiability and goodness, an *Eastern nature*; he can
> also hardly, a deposed Indian Sovereign, *not very* fond of the British
> rule as represented by the East India Company, and, above all, im-
> patient of Sir John Logan's tutorship, be expected to *like* to hear
> his country-people called *fiends* and monsters, and to see them brought
> in hundreds, if not thousands, to be executed.
>
> His best course is to say nothing, she must think. It is a great
> mercy that he, poor boy, is not there.

XI

OCTOBER–NOVEMBER

The Grapes of Wrath

SEPTEMBER BURNED ITSELF out, completing the record of an average temperature through three months considerably higher than anything known during eighty-six years of observation. London, as one said, began to fill up again. Jane Welsh Carlyle returned from Scotland to find that the dog Nero and the canaries had been cared for, and that her husband had got on better without her than her vanity, as she confessed, had led her to expect. He would keep opening windows, however, which gave her a succession of colds. Macaulay came back from his tour of the Moselle Valley, the Rhineland and the Tyrol to delight afresh in his Holly Lodge gardens, where the turf was still emerald though the flowers were less brilliant than when he went away. All the lands through which he had been travelling, he decided, "could not show such a carpet of soft, rich green herbage as mine."

A further satisfaction, indulged on his way from the station to Campden Hill, was a call at the Royal Institution to see what the papers had said about his peerage while he was away.

> There is a general cry of pleasure at my elevation. I am truly gratified by finding how well I stand with the public, and gratified by finding that Palmerston has made a hit for himself in bestowing this dignity on me.

Palmerston's hits were made all round the wicket, but his Day of Humiliation gained no applause from Macaulay. There was wind and rain on that 7 October, and the new Peer was not feeling well. However, he went to church, and heard a sermon that seized the opportunity to call for greater exertions to plant Christianity in India. "Ignorance, stupidity, bigotry," fumed Macaulay, whose key performance twenty years earlier—in the introduction to India of western higher education in the English language—had not been intended to smooth the path for dogma.

He trusted to the good sense of the country to reject "the maxims of this fool, and of others like him." But he trusted still more to its nonsense. Suddenly there seemed a great security against official proselytising in the unreconciled warfare of the sects.

It was a great day for the rhetoric of Evangelism and Dissent —which was one reason why the Queen would have preferred a Sunday, with the Established Church in fuller control. As it was, she attended no service at Balmoral, though no doubt it was kept as a quiet day. The Bishop of London, who was in the Highlands, found no demand there for the ministrations of which his own see was deprived, and the Archbishop of Canterbury also remained in the background. The Church Missionary Society, whose annual contributions from Northern India were reported to be endangered to the tune of £10,000, had got out an advance manifesto with hints for preachers struggling with an exotic theme; *The Times* printed twenty-six columns of extracts from the day's sermons; and Spurgeon drew a paying audience of twenty-two thousand to the Crystal Palace, which would have been closed on a Sunday. In the "congenial company," as it was tartly noted, "of Aphrodite Callipygos, the gods of Greece and the grim demons of Assyria and Egypt," as also of "the fountains, the veal-pie and lobster-salads, and the flower-pots," this mammoth act of humiliation grossed £1,100 for the management, out of which £200 went to the relief of sufferers by the Mutiny.

The recommended form of Anglican service, on sale at a penny with the evening papers of the previous day, had been thoughtfully prepared. There was the Intercession:

> Defend, we beseech Thee, our countrymen from the malice and treachery of the sons of violence who have risen up against them. Rebuke the madness of the people and stay the hand of the destroyer . . . Direct the counsels of those who rule in this hour of danger. Teach the natives of British India to prize the benefits which Thy good Providence has given them through the supremacy of this Christian land . . .

Jeremiah admonished the Lord's people in the First Lesson, and in the Second from St Luke, Jesus exonerated those eighteen upon whom the tower in Siloam had fallen. This was a clear summons to search within: "I tell you, Nay: but, except ye repent, ye shall all likewise perish." National sin, one preacher

Ah Moon of my delight who knowest no wane,
The Moon of Heaven is rising once again:
How oft hereafter rising shall she look
Through this same garden after me — in vain.

75

And when Thyself with shining foot shall pass
Among the guests star-scattered on the grass,
And in thy joyous errand reach the spot
Where I made one — turn down an empty glass!

TAMAM SHUD

FitzGerald's *Rubaiyat of Omar Khayyam*. A page from the copy made by
William Morris for Georgiana Burne-Jones in 1872. Calligraphy on
vellum by Morris; the two standing figures, and the seated figure
in lower border, designed by Morris; others by Burne-Jones. Figures
painted by Charles Fairfax-Murray

Rossetti: Study for Guinevere in the Oxford Union mural
Lancelot at the Shrine of the San Graal

Rossetti: *St Cecilia*, for Moxon's illustrated edition of *Poems by Alfred Tennyson*, 1857

Rossetti: self-caricature, mourning the death of his pet wombat in 1869

emphasised, "is but the aggregate of individual sin; and pride, and unbelief, and lust, and covetousness, and sloth, and malice— ay, these are very common things." A nation that had applauded *La Traviata*, and weakened the marriage-tie, and tolerated the blatancy of wealth and the misery of poverty, had much to answer for.

Privately it might be reflected that the feelings provoked by sepoy villainies testified in themselves to a fall from grace. Macaulay had remarked to a friend that "the account of that dreadful military execution at Peshawar—forty men blown at once from the mouths of cannon, their heads, legs, arms flying in all directions—was read with delight by people who three weeks ago were against all capital punishment." Publicly it was apparent that in Britain the executioner remained busy and indispensable. Madeleine Smith had made her glamorous escape from his attentions, but the supply of spectacular homicides showed no abatement. In September Henry Rogers, the master of a ship, had been hanged in Liverpool for a series of nauseating and finally fatal cruelties practised on a boy at sea, and the scenes at the scaffold had been described with the usual zest. The "Christian firmness" of the brute's repentance drew widely quoted comments from the hangman, the chaplain and the Under-Sheriff, to whom it was "just what you might expect from a British sailor and a Christian facing death."

It was all a little muddled, but with a fresh epidemic of murders even the *Saturday Review* was "tempted to say that, just when we are congratulating ourselves that we are not as other men . . . these things in Christian England are a hint to look at home . . . Fierce passion is much the same among us as in the tropics, and at all events our separate murderers have not the stimulus afforded by a frenzied multitude." The discovery on 9 October, on one of the buttresses of Waterloo Bridge, of a carpet-bag containing the mutilated and headless body of a gentleman, suggested at first the special interposition of Providence: since any other bridge, or any other part of that one, would have allowed the evidence of crime to drop safely to the bed of the Thames. Even so the gruesome mystery was destined to remain unsolved.

In the meantime there were signs of a revival of that expectation of divine displeasure which the aberrant comet had disappointed. Cholera, reported from Hamburg, might well be on its way to chastise both the moral and the sanitary delinquencies which had been so little repaired since the visitation of two years before. Precautionary advice had been duly sent out to the local Boards of Health, but there was little confidence that London's basic problems could be solved by exhortation, still less by the construction—which had been seriously proposed—of two huge and open cloacal ditches. There was something almost apocalyptic, also, in the worst of a mounting series of railway accidents, most of them on the Great Western. While all of them were blamed upon inefficiencies and economies designed to save the shareholders' dividends at a particularly bad time, a head-on crash in South Wales, with much loss of life, was frankly compared to one of the famous "Mad Martin's" canvases of cosmic catastrophe.

From America there had come some premonitory talk of a run on the banks, of a kind unlikely to please anyone except Karl Marx and Friedrich Engels. And there had been a sequence of setbacks, which even Greville noticed as remarkable, in the great march of progress. Towards the end of August the submarine telegraph cable to America, on which such wonderful hopes had been set by shareholders and philosophers, was lost in deep water when the operation seemed close to completion. Early in October the giant new bell in the Parliament Tower, already dubbed Big Ben, was found to be seriously cracked. And on 3 November the eagerly awaited public event of the launching of the *Great Eastern* faded into anti-climax when, "by an unaccountable mistake of some workmen in slackening a chain they were told to tighten," the monster remained as stranded at Millwall as the January whale had been at Winterton. Brunel's vessel had, in fact, been re-named *Leviathan*. And the *Record*, pointing out the profanity of lifting from the Scriptures "a synonym for the Devil," went on to show how "the great Leviathan no sooner receives its most inauspicious, repulsive name than Providence puts a hook in its nose and forbids it to proceed any further on its way."

What next was one to say of the Bengal tiger which by some means found itself at large in the City, and mauled an innocent boy before it could be captured? And under what ill star were Mr and Mrs Gladstone roused in the early hours of 29 October by the clanging bell and thundering hooves of the Chester Fire Brigade, to watch the dreadful burning of Hawarden Church—

by arson, it was thought, and "done with diabolical care and skill"—just after the completion of the restorations for which the family had with difficulty found the funds?

Yet Providence had not exhausted the singular favours that it had to bestow. From Norfolk to Sussex a tremendous downpour on 22 October did something to restore the necessary balance of rainfall, and thereafter the countryside basked in a radiant autumnal smile. Nathaniel Hawthorne, who had reached Coventry in his ranging travels, watched with admiration the care with which the harvest of falling leaves was swept up and carried off in wheelbarrows, for tidiness and for compost; but he was surprised that "the pastures look just as green as ever—a deep, bright verdure, that seems almost sunshine itself." Accepting it all, after a year in Britain, as the normality of an under-rated climate, he remarked on 27 October that suburban flower-beds "might still do credit to an American midsummer . . . and I have no doubt that the old year's flowers will bloom till those of the new year appear. Really, the English winter is not so terrible as ours."

On the next day Ruskin, rising early as always at Denmark Hill, recorded: "A grey morning with filmy tracery of hair-cloud. Heavy dew. White horizontal mist among trees in valley; opens into soft blue sky with *cirri* and quiet air." And at Leamington it broadened for Hawthorne into "the most beautiful of all days, and gilded almost throughout with the precious English sunshine—the most delightful sunshine ever made." Two lovely mornings followed, inspiring Ruskin to make a sketch—"soft and clear, and warm days, and noble sunsets with heaped clouds."

Well might there be such noble sunsets. Well might there be, in the dawn of the month's last day, "bright sunshine on the dew; a little cold; a bird or two twittering." And well might Macaulay, on the arrival of news the more electrifying for the nervous six weeks of its transit, reach for his own notebook:

October 27:— Huzza! Huzza! Thank God! Delhi is taken. A great event. Glorious to the nation, and one which will resound through all Christendom and Islam. What an exploit for that handful of Englishmen in the heart of Asia to have performed!

Throughout the land the newspapers took their tremendous cue. In his Scottish home at Hartrigge Lord Campbell had been brooding at night on the envy and ill will of his foes and critics, and resolving not to add to the number of authors who, he read, "died of a broken heart, by reason of unjust attacks upon their writings." In the morning came the news of Delhi, and he measured his elation by certain dire contingencies that he had been contemplating for months: the end of empire, the slaughter of every European in India, to be followed by fearful dangers nearer home. "In two years a regiment of Cossacks might have been bivouacking at Hartrigge."

In lower Hampstead Marx was deep in "the American crisis which we predicted in November 1850." But he could spare a thought for "the traditional English good luck" in India. Engels, recovering in Jersey, had further comments:

> It is probable that the sepoys made a poor defence of the walls of Delhi. It was above all house-to-house fighting, and there is every reason to think that the English must have put native troops in the forefront . . .
> The American crisis is superb, and not near its end . . . The effect in England seems to have begun already with the Borough Bank in Liverpool. So much the better. Business will be paralyzed from now for two or three months. Now we shall have a chance.

If anything, after the ill-success of Mr Gladstone and Bishop Wilberforce, could restore purity, tenderness and dignity to Christian matrimony it was surely the rites that were in preparation for the Princess Royal. The Queen and her family, however, had not long been back in Windsor Castle when the Earl of Clarendon communicated a proposal to which she took the strongest exception. He had heard from the British Minister to Prussia that feeling at that Court favoured Berlin rather than London as the place where the marriage, appointed for next January, should fitly be celebrated. The bride's mother expressed herself in a short torrent of underlinings and capitals:

> The assumption of its being *too much* for a Prince Royal of Prussia to *come* over to marry *the Princess Royal of Great Britain* IN England is too *absurd*, to say the least . . . Whatever may be the usual practice of Prussian Princes, it is not *every* day that one marries the eldest daughter of the Queen of England. The question therefore must be considered as settled and closed . . .

Settled and closed it was. National humiliation was an indulgence that could be carried too far.

So far as appearances went—and they went a long way—
nobody would have guessed that that other redoubt, the household of Charles Dickens, was not holding out: nobody, that is,
except two or three close friends and the trusted servant Anne,
now the housekeeper at Tavistock House, who could hardly
have misinterpreted the instructions she had received by post
from Dickens in September. She was to have in a carpenter to
close up the doorway which communicated in the London house
between the marital bed-chamber and the master's dressing
room, and to fill the space with white deal shelves protected by
a cupboard-door. A single iron bedstead and the requisite bedding
had been ordered for the converted dressing-room, and nothing
must be said by anybody.

It was only one half of a separation *a mensa et thoro*, but it
was as final in its significance as a divorce *a vinculo matrimonii*.
The summer of Gad's Hill the long-desired, Gad's Hill the
freshly-possessed, was over. The winter return to Tavistock
House was to be made, for the time being, under the guise of
propriety, the genial host still entertaining as necessary beside
the dutiful but colourless hostess, and no word about the up-
stairs conversion. No word, either, about Ellen Ternan: or not
to Forster, the friend of the long married years who now, since
Collins was not very serious about such subjects, was needed
again as a confidant. The confession to Forster was in the terms
that any man, in or out of fiction, might employ to justify and
condemn himself at the same time. "Poor Catherine and I were
not made for each other, and there is no help for it." But poor
Charles would make no maudlin complaint, nor disguise from
himself—he repeatedly insisted—what might be urged from the
other side:

God knows she would have been a thousand times happier if she
had married another kind of man, and that her avoidance of this
destiny would have been at least equally good for us both. I am often
cut to the heart by thinking what a pity it is, for her own sake, that
I ever fell in her way; and if I were sick and disabled tomorrow,
I know how sorry she would be, and how deeply grieved myself,
to think how we had lost each other. But exactly the same
incompatibility would arise, the moment I was well again . . .
Her temperament will not go with mine . . . What is now befal-
ling me I have seen steadily coming on, ever since the days you
remember . . .

Holman Hunt at this time was in equal need of a marriage counsellor. Only he wanted in, not out. He was in such a state that a visit to the Manchester Exhibition had sent him "quite crazy" with love for a whole line of feminine sitters to Reynolds and Gainsborough and other masters. Though ready to admit that the infatuation of Pygmalion might prompt a desperate vow to die a bachelor, he warned the Coombes at Oxford, the solicitous friends of several artists besides himself that he would be coming to consult them on a subject that must be decided one way or the other. "Beg Mrs Coombe," he added, "not to be alarmed at this notion. I have not committed myself."

But he had committed himself, so far as would eventually serve the purposes of blackmail. He was still seized of the project of educating Annie Miller to the standards required of a presentable wife. He was also searching, with the help of a friend as go-between, for some lodging for Annie more seemly than the grim warren behind the Cross Keys. Posing for Hunt, however, was not Annie's idea of a full and beautiful life, and her supplementary pleasures had fallen off when the grouse began to call to Lord Ranelagh. By all accounts there was more fun to be had, of the Bohemian kind she knew and enjoyed, in Oxford of the Long Vacation than in London of the steamy recess. So Hunt was put off by a letter feigning illness, and Annie Miller appeared suddenly among the artists in the Oxford High. Her stay was a short one, but exhilarating for all concerned. Back in London, her excuse of illness now involved her in a visit with the anxious Hunt to a specialist, who "gave a very favourable verdict." A respectable boarding-house had by this time been found for her in Pimlico, complete with a retired schoolmistress in another room whom Hunt engaged to continue her education. Neither the landlady nor the schoolmistress, it later turned out, were too respectable to supplement their modest receipts with the *douceurs* with which Annie's gentlemen callers rewarded their discretion.

The jovial crew in Oxford, their operations interminably extended, had other visitors. One was Coventry Patmore, who wrote them up richly for the *Saturday Review*, though his article did not appear until Christmas week: by which time the brilliance of colour which so pleased him—the "voluptuous radiance of variegated tints," making the walls look like "the margins of a highly-illuminated manuscript"—was already at the mercy of the flaking distemper. Four of the bays were as yet completely blank, but nothing seemed to quench the exuberance of the band of brothers. As long as any of them lived, though all should be forgot, they would remember with advantages what feats they did, under what mysteriously inspired leadership, in 1857.

It was all getting well beyond Ruskin, who came and praised some of the work, but complained that "one can't get them to be quiet at it, or resist a fancy . . . away they go to jingle, jingle, without ever caring what o'clock it is." He was distinctly irritated to find how difficult it was to manage them. It was also, for a stunner who happened to catch their eye, difficult to resist them. The dark-haired beauty of Jane Burden, discovered in the audience at the Oxford theatre (or in church, ran another version), not only caused the features of Lizzie Siddal in Rossetti's Guinevere to be repainted, but to some extent changed the Pre-Raphaelite archetype. "I cannot paint you, but I love you," wrote Morris on the back of his canvas, and turned it to her as the whole group sat sketching her portrait. By marrying Morris, Jane was to preserve herself for Rossetti with the ineffable attraction of the not quite attainable.

Through the Long Vacation they had been able to isolate themselves in the little world of their own making. With the return of the students, when they had to move from the High Street to a different lodging, they attracted undergraduate attention and one or two new friends. Now it was Swinburne, hopping about Oxford like some small, nervous, fire-crested bird, who was caught in Gabriel's net. As to painting he was a non-playing member, but "dear little Carrots," as Burne-Jones called him, entered instantly into their ardours and frivolities, penetrated the dream with his own deviant intensity, and listened as rapt as any when Gabriel Rossetti talked or Topsy Morris gave them another grind from the bundled brief of his *Defence of Guinevere*.

> Pray but one prayer for me 'twixt thy closed lips;
> Think but one thought of me up in the stars.
> The summer night waneth, the morning light slips
> Faint and grey 'twixt the leaves of the aspen,
>   betwixt the cloud-bars . . .

Ford Madox Brown, who had been persuaded to go to Manchester just before the Exhibition closed, descended also upon Oxford, whence he wrote bibulously to his wife, at one a.m. on the first of November, that they were "All very jolly here" and "Lots of good fellows of all sorts here." But he was too old at the game to join in. The eighty-foot ladders were too high, and the rewards by way of expenses too low, despite the daily fare of "roast beef, a plum-pudding each, and old ale." Rossetti himself was coming to realise that cash-crops were better than subsistence-farming. He gave more time to watercolours and less to the murals, and would dart up to London to keep his contacts warm. On 5 November he and Hunt were both guests at the London house of that vivid lady Julia Cameron and her jurist husband. Her enthusiasms had not yet embraced photography, but they did embrace Mr and Mrs Tennyson, who were staying with her after their Lakeland holiday. Edward Lear, who had spent the summer in Ireland, was also there for the evening, which he improved by singing at the piano, to his own settings, a choice of Tennyson's lyrics. When the party had broken up the family and their house-guests settled down to listen to the poet himself, reading his *Morte d'Arthur* in his organ-voice.

Once more the Round Table was like to be dissolved. It may be that Lizzie's instincts had warned her that Gabriel was enjoying his freedom more than he should, or perhaps she was in clinical fact as ill as the situation required. Either way the message that reached Gabriel was of a desperate case. On 14 November he packed up and left Oxford for Matlock, and without him the campaign dwindled to its end. "They're all the least bit crazy," muttered Ruskin, as he went back to his cataloguing of the Turners. He had lectures for South Kensington to work on as well.

It was a grave theme that Ruskin proposed to examine: *The Deteriorative Power of Conventional Art over Nations.* It was also a topical one:

> Since the race of man began its course on this earth, nothing has ever been done by it so significative of all bestial, and lower than bestial, degradation as the acts of the Indian in the year that has just passed by . . . Cruelty stretched to its fiercest against the gentle and unoffending, and corruption festering to its loathsomest in the midst of the witnessing presence of a disciplined civilization, these we could not have known to be within the practical compass of human guilt, but for the acts of the mutineer . . .

More news came in as he framed his rolling periods, news that Macaulay could not ignore on 11 November:

Huzza! Good news! Lucknow relieved ... God be praised! Another letter from Longman. They have already sold 7,600 more copies. This is near £6,000, as I reckoned, in my pocket. But it gratified me, I am glad to be able to say with truth, far, very far, less than the Indian news. I could hardly eat my dinner for joy.

In the week preceding this ecstatic day London had had its first winter fogs, but on the tenth, as Nathaniel Hawthorne and his wife travelled up from Leamington, they had seen "everywhere the immortal verdure of England, scarcely less perfect than in June, so far as the fields are concerned." The dawn of good tidings, as Ruskin saw it from his South London garden, came up with orange brightness at the horizon, the sky above it passing through greenish amber into purple, the morning star large like a cross, but dwindling to a point as the day rose. There was a heavy dew, turning to early mist, but the air was quite mild and birds were singing. By ten o'clock the sun was warm "on the arbutus' scarlet berries and white blossoms, and coral of the holly, the fuchsias still in flower: leaves full and even green on many trees." From morning to evening it was a fine and sparkling day.

Could one imagine a race of men who had wilfully cut themselves off from all enjoyment of the matchless beauty of the natural world, and from all possible sources of healthy knowledge? Ruskin could, if the effort were demanded of him. The faculty of discerning a nation's moral standing through its art, and of forecasting its art from a view of its morals, had laid upon him, at this point in time and space, a critical responsibility. The great 1851 Exhibition, on which he had maintained a virtual and eloquent silence, had revealed to some members of Prince Albert's team certain unsuspected virtues in its Indian section: a novelty of invention, mobility within flat design, a language of abstract motives as against the abundantly representational ornament of Europe. Unconvinced in the Crystal Palace, Ruskin had almost nowhere else to look. Even if he carried his taste for illuminated manuscripts to the Moghul miniatures in the Royal collections, he would find them generally identified as Persian. Only in 1857, only with the fortnightly despatches in *The Times*, the published letters from private sources, would light break upon the subject of India, and thus upon the recondite consideration of its arts.

It broke. From vermilion daysprings beyond the rising ground

of Norwood, from ethereal distances in the watercolours of
Turner, Ruskin turned to dwell for his lecture on what Indian
art must indicate of the people who practised it:

> Over the whole spell of creation they have thrown a veil in which
> there is no rent. For them no star peeps through the blanket of
> the dark; for them neither their heaven shines, nor their mountains
> rise; for them the flowers do not blossom; for them the creatures
> of field and forest do not live. They lie bound in the dungeon
> of their own conception, encompassed only by doleful phantoms,
> or by spectral vacancy.

No such traumatic involvement betrayed Tennyson. The little
rocking-horse exercise of *Havelock's March* was not to be retained
for his collected poems, and two whole decades were allowed for
the recollection in tranquillity of the Banner of England in *The
Defence of Lucknow*. Camelot and Lyonesse were perhaps his
realms of escape from the friendly remark of FitzGerald that
he ought to have been a dragoon. Back at Farringford, whence
he had watched the transports for the Crimea going down
Channel, the Laureate acceded to the Queen's request for two
new verses for the National Anthem, to be used at the marriage
of the Princess Royal: *God bless our Prince and Bride* . . .

Something of the Mutiny Summer had certainly wrought upon
Charles Kingsley. No marginal *graffiti* could exorcise the hellish
visitants that mopped and mowed about Eversley as the Rector
prepared his sermons for the troops on embarkation call who
came over from Portsmouth and Southampton. When he bolted
his study-door one afternoon, remaining inaccessible until
dinner-time, what he brought down to read to his guests, the
paper as yet undried in his hand, was *The Last Buccanier*, an
irresistible excursion among his Spanish Main fantasies:

> Oh sweet it was in Avès to hear the landward breeze,
> A-swing with good tobacco in a net between the trees,
> With a negro lass to fan you, while you listened to the roar
> Of the breakers on the reef outside, that never touched
>   the shore . . .

But what he loosed upon the world towards the end of the year,
in *Andromeda and Other Poems*, was the piece called *Saint Maura*
in blank verse, of which he confessed:

I can hardly bear to read it myself, but it is the deepest and clearest thing I have ever done . . . It caused me during writing—it was all done in a day and a night—a poetic fervour such as I have never felt before or since.

The theme had been provided by the Rector's compulsive readings in the early martyrologies, "a sort of inspiration which I could not resist," in a story which "has always been my *experimentum crucis* of the false connection between martyrdom and celibacy."

One can see what he meant. But observe the context: a male and a female martyr crucified side by side, she hopefully pregnant by him, he with his eyes gouged out. The poem is her monologue to him, her subjective account of the temptation, after they had blinded him, to renounce Christ as the means of saving him from further and nameless tortures; then of his fierce rebuke of her contemplated apostasy, so that her madness snapped and all was clear, as with downcast eyes she defied their persecutors:

> "She knows what shame is still; so strip her." "Ah!"
> I shrieked, "Not that, Sir! Any pain! So young
> I am—a wife too—I am not my own,
> But his—my husband's!" But they took my shawl,
> And tore my tunic off, and there I stood
> Before them all . . . Husband! You love me still?

After that exposure, uninterrupted by the looked-for earthquake, nothing that might be inflicted would be unbearable.

> Once only—once, when first I felt the whip—
> It coiled so keen around my side, and sent
> A fire-flash through my heart which choked me—then
> I shrieked—that once. The foolish echo rang
> So far and long—I prayed you might not hear.

And so at length she was taken to the place of crucifixion.

> . . . As I lay
> Beneath your feet, while they were binding me,
> I knew I was forgiven then! When I cried
> "Here am I, husband! The lost lamb returned,
> All re-baptised in blood!" and you said, "Come!

Come to thy bride-bed, martyr, wife once more!"
From that same moment all my pain was gone;
And ever since those sightless eyes have smiled
Love—Love!

Perused between vengeful editorials and the kind of correspondence from India on which the Queen commented "The
horrors of shame and every outrage that women must most
dread . . . should never have been made known . . . it was a
great mercy *all* were *killed*"—consumed thus, *Saint Maura* was
quite a dish.

"Is it possible," Macaulay had been asking himself, "that a
year passed under the influence of such feelings should not have
some effect on the national character?" In September, when the
outcome in India had seemed to many to be so precariously
balanced, he had drawn on his customary detachment to conclude
that the effect would be partly good and partly bad.

> The nerves of our minds will be braced. Effeminate, mawkish
> philanthropy will lose all its influence. But shall we not hold human
> life generally cheaper than we have done? Having brought ourselves
> to exult in the misery of the guilty, shall we not feel less sympathy
> for the sufferings of the innocent?

In the person of the century's most devoted and effective philanthropist, however, the quality on display was not effeminate
and mawkish but muscular and militant. As associated in the
Earl of Shaftesbury with political conservatism and Christian
Evangelism, the strain was of peculiar virulence when applied to
the scene of British dominion in India. Had that country been
"ravaged with fire and sword to make proselytes," Shaftesbury
felt entitled to ask, "could we have excited a more savage
rebellion, a more awful insurrection, than this which has been
wrought by these fondled and ungrateful Sepoys?" No? Then
let us, setting aside the horrors of the event, "rejoice in it as the
greatest that has yet occurred for the benefit of civilization since
we first planted our feet in the territories of the East."

Such was his approach in the powerful oration which he
delivered at Wimborne, in aid of a fund for the sufferers which
had been making (according to Greville) much less progress
than any of the appeals organised during the Crimean War. By
now the God of Battles could be seen to have declared himself

in the recapture of Delhi; but the horrors could by no means be set aside, and Shaftesbury's thesis must incline him to make the most of them. This he did with such incautious zeal that he had afterwards to confess, under pressure, to "an inaccuracy in the heat of speaking."

He had accepted, at second or third hand, an unauthenticated report of the mutilation of British women, citing as his authority Lady Canning, the wife of the Governor-General. The story as it got about—and Shaftesbury seems to have given it further countenance at Exeter Hall—pictured refugee ladies reaching Calcutta without breasts, and in other cases without hands or arms. Though the platform version confined itself, as reported, to the loss of noses, it was enough to draw the dry attention of Disraeli, who a few weeks later happened to travel to Hatfield in the same carriage as Lady Canning's mother. After indignantly denying her daughter's complicity in spreading the groundless rumour, the lady spoke of letters which had poured in, following Shaftesbury's speech, to the Ladies' Committee for the Relief of the Indian [*sic*] Sufferers, of which she was a member. To Disraeli the whole business was something to be shared with Mrs Brydges Williams in his next letter:

> A surgeon wrote . . . stating that he had great experience in the formation of artificial noses, that he was ready to give all his skill, time, and devotion, to the cause, but as the machinery was rather expensive, he hoped, in accepting his services, the Committee would defray the prime cost of the springs! He then gave a tariff of prices, and offered to supply noses for English ladies by the dozen, and, I believe, even by the gross . . .

Stanchlessly, as if an artery had been severed, the flow of words from the daily and weekly Press treated as inexhaustible the subject of a dependency to which the late Duke of Wellington had once complained that it was impossible to draw public notice. It is not easy to explain a gnawing fear lest the fractional British forces, marching at a hundred and fifteen in the shade, fighting against enormous odds, and directly aware of the ferocity of their opponents, should prove inappropriately merciful. But the order of General Wilson for the Delhi assault—"No quarter for the mutineers, spare the women and children"—was not enough for *The Times*, which demanded that the city be razed to the ground after "every tree and gable-end" had served as a gibbet.

It was the Governor-General's Order-in-Council for the avoidance of *indiscriminate* executions which first gained him the opprobrious title of "Clemency Canning." Reported in England in October—after the news of the massacres of Europeans at Cawnpore but before that of the re-taking of Delhi—the Order (miscalled a Proclamation) provided the target of concentration which the Press, or a great part of it, had needed. The bloodshot mood of the Calcutta Europeans, of which much of the feeling in England was a fairly faithful reflection, had been reported to Queen Victoria by Canning as a matter of grave concern:

> The cry is raised loudest by those who have been sitting quietly in their homes from the beginning and have suffered little from the convulsions around them, unless it be in pocket. It is to be feared that this feeling of exasperation will be a great impediment in the way of restoring tranquillity and good order.

The Queen did not fail to reply, writing on 9 November, that she deeply deplored the excesses of bitterness that were being poured out upon her Indian subjects. The Governor-General was told at the same time how strongly she felt the injustice of the newspaper attacks upon himself. To these he professed "an indifference so complete as to surprise himself," but he was by no means indifferent, even if he did not say so to the Queen, to the stony silence of Lord Palmerston and the absence of any expression of Government support for their chief executive in India in these trying times.

Support for the man on the spot—as in the glaring instance of Bowring in the Chinese business—was a virtue that Palmerston often carried to a fault. But in this case he was not ill pleased that public indignation should spend itself upon the conduct of affairs in Calcutta rather than in London. With Parliament in recess he felt no compulsion to intervene, until increasing pressure from his scandalised colleagues persuaded him to choose a moment and an occasion—the Lord Mayor's dinner on 9 November—when the baying for Canning's blood had just begun to slacken and the better news from India gave him the chance as Prime Minister to stand forth as the unruffled helmsman in the terrible tempest. The amends to Canning were made handsomely, thought Greville, who had himself been pressing for them. In other respects, he added, the old champion's speech was "full of jactance and bow-wow, but well enough calculated to draw cheers from a miscellaneous audience."

Fresh strawberries and raspberries in November, and Pam in his evergreen form. The year's magic was still at work. Nothing could avert the self-engendered fogs of a London winter, but even these were interrupted by an occasional sparkling day, and to the exploring Hawthorne there were times when fog itself seemed to spiritualise the dense activities of the endless streets. He wandered everywhere, diligently exhausting every ancient and recommended sight, and then making for Billings-gate and Smithfield Markets or St Katherine's Docks; observing organ-grinders, barrow-boys, oyster-stands, pedlars, crossing-sweepers, ragged and dirty children at play; astounded to pass from dimness and squalor into the Temple Gardens, gorgeous with chrysanthemums, to move into the Inns of Court "out of an age of weekdays condensed into the present hour, into what seems an eternal sabbath." He was caught, and enjoyed being caught, between a thrill of admiration for "that grand lullaby, the roar of the City," and a chilling sense of enormity in the whole phenomenon, of being "surrounded by materialisms and hemmed in with the grossness of this earthly existence."

For the gross operators themselves, however, November turned as treacherous as a sepoy. Shock-waves from the American upheaval were answering Marx's happy predictions with the rumble of stricken banks and tottering business houses. The Bank of England rate stood on 4 November at nine per cent, the point that it had touched in the crisis of 1847. A week later the pressure-gauge rose to ten per cent and Palmerston had to tell the Queen that the Reserve Fund was so low that the Bank would have been unable to meet the calls upon it without special powers to exceed the statutory limits of its issues against bullion. These powers had consequently been authorised, in a letter to the Governor of the Bank of England from the Prime Minister and the Chancellor of the Exchequer, in time to avert a general panic before the Stock Exchange closed its day's business; and there had been no time to take Her Majesty's pleasure in the matter.

The device had worked in 1847. But in 1857 so many closed questions had been opened, so many unthinkable things had been thought, so many sage provisions had failed of their effect

and so many unexpected accidents had redressed the balance
that there was simply no telling. Where was certainty, when the
Apocalypse itself had proved unreliable? Under the title *An
End to Everything*, a contributor to *Punch* put the feeling into
verse:

> Hope, where wilt thou cast thine anchor?
>   Faith, where wilt thou make thy nest?
> If we cannot trust our banker,
>   Where is confidence to rest?
>
> Earth below will seem forsaken,
>   Sky appear a blank above,
> When Commercial Credit's shaken,
>   Who will dream of Woman's Love?

If the wombat had an answer, there was nobody through whom
he could communicate. Gabriel Rossetti remained for the present in Matlock, suffering for the sin of Sir Lancelot, and there
were no more assignations at the wombat's lair. Lewis Carroll,
released for a week-end from Oxford because St Andrew's Day
fell on Monday, the last day of November, spent much of that
overcast and windy day in the Zoological Gardens, but missed
the chance of making an acquaintance that might have promised
much. For the ground of his mind was already partly occupied.
A fortnight earlier he had found, in a reproduction in Oxford of
Landseer's painting *Titania*, some wonderful points for attention
—"the white rabbit especially."

XII

DECEMBER

Ring Out the Wombat

THE FINANCIAL CYCLONE that had threatened the City and the nation spun slowly away. Suspension of the Bank Charter Act had its effect. The fears that French policies would move out of line, and that the American President would repudiate treaty obligations towards Britain, were alike proved groundless. Yet Karl Marx did not despair. "Despite all my financial embarrassment," he had written to Engels, who was now back in Manchester, "I have never, since 1849, felt so much pleasure as over the explosion of this crisis."

It was the inner contradictions that sustained him. Whatever Governments and National Banks might do to manipulate the situation, the evidence in the world's foremost trading and industrial nation was that production had necessarily been cut back, unemployment and short-time work on reduced wages were increasing, prices were falling and so must the revenue. This was enough already to raise a clamour that India must bear the expenses of repressing the rebellion. There would thus have been much to justify revolutionary optimism, but for those characteristics of the British proletariat which nearly a decade ago had plunged Marx into a misery of frustration and contempt. The enquiries which Greville, from a different viewpoint, had been making among his knowledgeable cronies pointed indeed to "a very hard and hungry winter for the working classes, vast numbers of people being already out of employment." But if the reports reaching him from one distressed area, that of Lancashire, were anything to go by, Britain could take it.

There was no disaffection or bad feeling towards the upper classes and employers; workpeople seemed to have greatly improved in good sense and reflection, and were satisfied of the sympathy felt for them, and the disposition entertained by the rich to do all in their power to alleviate the distress of the poor . . . This moral condition of the labouring classes is a most satisfactory sign of the times.

Palmerston's emergency action, however, entailed—as he had indicated to the Queen—"one very inconvenient consequence." It would be constitutionally necessary that Parliament, still resting from its prolonged labours of the summer, should be summoned to take cognizance of the steps taken and pass an Act of Indemnity. By arranging for this tiresome Session to be opened by the Queen on 3 December, its deliberations could at present be confined to ten days or so by the Christmas recess; but there would be no repetition of last winter, when the Government had had a free toboggan-ride into two distant wars and a number of nearer convulsions. Even a few pre-Christmas sittings would enable its opponents to move beyond the business of the Bank Charter Act, towards topics which it would have been preferable to postpone until February at soonest. Questions were bound to be asked about the still vague promises of further franchise Reform; about the Government's handling of the Indian crisis, now that returns had confirmed the obstinate insistence of those who conceived steam to be faster than sail; and about the changes which must obviously be drawing near in the anomalous double responsibility of the Government and the East India Company. On this latter subject, besides submitting some of his own ideas to the Queen, Palmerston had in the anxious days of September asked his Foreign Secretary Clarendon to let his mind dwell while at the shaving-mirror, or on a country walk. "He has a jolly way of looking at disasters," wrote Clarendon to his wife.

So the Queen, who had already noted in her diary "a general feeling that India shd. belong to *me*," rode in her coach to the House of Lords and delivered the re-opening speech that Palmerston had composed. Hawthorne, who had hoped to see her pass by but failed to be there on time, contented himself with the pealing bells of St Margaret's and St Martin's ("London seems to cry out through them, and did homage to the Queen"). Lady Charlotte Schreiber, who did see her pass by, found the whole thing very quiet, and the onlookers apathetic. Nor was the ten days' Session remarkably lively, apart from some premature attempts to apportion praise and censure in respect of the Indian affair.

The Chief Justice, however, feeling satisfied as to the "most brilliant success" of his Obscenity Act, was looking for a chance of "annoying Brougham and Lyndhurst" by waving the thing once more under their antagonistic noses. He had even persuaded himself that "the French police, roused by the accounts of what we are now doing, have been energetically employed in purifying the Palais Royal and the Rue Vivienne." If he was thinking of the August prosecution of Baudelaire on account of *Les Fleurs du Mal*, he had got it wrong. The reactionary drive in Paris had been evident in February, months before Lord Campbell's crusade, in the attempt to suppress Flaubert's *Madame Bovary*. It was because that case had gone against them that the French authorities had sought, found and convicted an alternative victim.

Because of that earlier failure, again, the *Saturday Review* was now able, though "not without considerable hesitation," to notice at some length an English translation of *Madame Bovary*. Subversive thoughts were still alive:

> We are by no means prepared to say that, in literature, emasculation produces purity . . . Whether a light literature entirely based upon love, and absolutely and systematically silent as to one most important side of it, may not have some tendency to stimulate passions to which it is far too proper ever to allude, is a question which is too wide for our limits on the present occasion. But it is one which we should do well to take into serious consideration before we preach the doctrine that the contemporaries of Mr Dickens have made a vast step in advance of the contemporaries of Mr Fielding.

The French novel—Lyndhurst's "whole flight from Crébillon *fils* to Paul de Kock"—might remain as the archetype of depravity. But the Lady of the Camellias herself, after troubling this whole year with her sinister ambience, had made an impudent escape from the closing net. A theatrical manager at Rochester having announced the production of a drama bearing her name, a remonstrance to the Lord Chamberlain was made by some alarmed members of the public. A copy of the play was therefore required from the manager, scrutinised by an official, and sent back with the comment:

> I have examined the drama entitled *The Lady of the Camellias*, and find it to correspond so nearly with the opera of *La Traviata*, which has been licensed by the Lord Chamberlain, that I shall not put any impediment in the way of your performing it at Rochester.

But the House of Lords must still witness Campbell's victory-lap. He did it by moving for a return of the seizures so far made under his Act. Half of the offending shops, he went on to claim, had closed down, and the remainder now dealt in nothing but moral and religious books. "Holywell Street, which had long set law and decency at defiance, has capitulated after several assaults." Just like Delhi, he managed to add. Nobody was blown from a gun, but in the end William Dugdale died in the House of Correction.

Death knew better than to be at home when Florence Nightingale called, and in the last weeks of this nonesuch year her calls had become insistent. There was nothing very odd, at thirty-seven, in making a will. But for a woman already trying to work herself into the ground the additional labour of composing posthumous letters went beyond necessity. Upon Sidney Herbert, who was very much nearer the grave, she had laid on 26 November the task of pressing forward the clean sweep in Army conditions which the great Report had demanded. "I hope," she wrote, "you will have no chivalrous ideas of what is 'due' to my 'memory.' The only thing that can be 'due' to me is what is good for the troops." And on 11 December she entrusted to her sister Parthenope directions for the manner of her burial. Rejecting as absurd the idea that the dead exist in some way where their remains have been deposited, she nevertheless desired that a grave for her should be found in the Crimea, among those of the men she could not save. In the meantime she had found for herself a deathbed from which to continue her commanding activity until well into the twentieth century.

In its own unconscionable way the long summer was also, even now, resisting extinction. In the Isle of Wight fuchsias were blooming, and raspberries were picked on 20 December. Gloucester had not only Christmas roses in flower, but primroses at the same time. It was a breakdown in familiar arrangements, rather than any hint of a cold spell, which made John Addington Symonds write home from Harrow, in his Sunday letter on 6 December: "I am in great want of my flannel drawers and cannot conceive why they have not come." And for his friend Pretor, the strange affections that the wanton breezes of May had stirred in his headmaster, could aspire in a mild December to the word in the ear and the hand on the thigh, the untranslatable Greek mood and the inescapable Victorian betrayal. It was

Symonds who innocently revealed the lapse that cost Dr Vaughan a bishopric.

"There are many kinds of temptation, Eric; many kinds. And they are easy to fall into." Stirred by the success of Hughes with *Tom Brown's Schooldays*, which had gone rollicking into its second edition, Frederick Farrar was already preparing the darker draught of *Eric, or Little By Little*, its encounters with sin and death so searing that particular precautions must be taken to deter identification of the school concerned. But here, at least, was one pool of contamination into which the heir to the throne had not been carelessly thrust. Returning from his Continental tour in October, the Prince of Wales had been subjected under his tutor to a régime of studies calculated to erase the memory of Königswinter and the squalid little debauch. Examined at Christmas, he showed symptoms of a sturdy rejection of Classical History, producing in answer to the entire paper just six-and-a-half tentative lines. His response to questions on English and Modern History was considerably brighter, but nobody thought of changing his curriculum.

Christmas Day dawned in serene weather and continued gloriously, like a fine day of spring. Ruskin, who had been languid and despondent after one of his colds, recovered his spirits and walked to Norwood through dry fields. George Eliot and Lewes, established at Richmond since July, had a clear view from the rolling parkland right across London to Hampstead—"so distinctly that it seemed to have suddenly come nearer to us. We ate our turkey together in a happy *solitude à deux*." And Charles Greville decided that the bright and balmy air was in splendid consonance with the news received on Christmas Eve from India: where, on 17 November, in the second and effective relief of Lucknow, Sir Colin Campbell had succeeded in bringing away the entire garrison of the Residency, with six hundred women and children and more than a thousand sick and wounded men. Nothing, however, could deflect Carlyle, who spent Christmas Day festooned in the latest batch of galley-proofs, from the glum observation that "all mortals are tumbling about in a state of drunken Saturnalia, delirium, or quasi-debauch, according to their several sects—a very strange method of thanking God for sending them a Redeemer."

Whether they were worth redeeming, the Sage did not fail to add, was another question. Nobody interrupted their celebrations to ask his opinion under this head, and the chosen champion of Christmas had lost his verve. Dickens had "never known a moment's peace or content," he told Wilkie Collins, "since the last night of *The Frozen Deep*."

For the now customary Christmas number of *Household Words* the Dickens-Collins collaboration had produced a story, *The Perils of Certain English Prisoners*, of small merit or interest save as an allegory—set in Central America in 1744—of the Indian drama of 1857. Elsewhere, and notably at Astley's Amphitheatre on the south side of the Thames, the season's entertainments brought sepoys and highlanders on the stage, "black rascals plotting," ladies rescued in the nick of time, realistic bangings and bayonetings, rumbles and explosions, until "the revenge of England comes down in a storm of fire that makes you smell powder for an hour afterwards." But there were no more Twelfth Night dramatics in the Dickens household, no more convivial parties at Tavistock House. Possessed by day with a sense of ineluctable change, Dickens dreamed at night of an endless perspective of barriers, over which he was required somehow to struggle with his hands and feet tightly bound.

It is a relief to turn to Friedrich Engels, surmounting every obstacle in pursuit of the fox in the neighbourhood of Manchester. Happily restored to health, he spent seven hours of Boxing Day in the saddle:

> Such a pleasure gives me each time, and for several days, a surexcitation of all the devils; but I know no physical pleasure to beat it . . . There were at least twenty falls, two horses were killed, and they killed a fox. I was in at the death . . . Good wishes to all the family for the revolutionary year 1858.

The roadside banks defy the calendar, with *alchemilla* and shepherd's purse in flower, a purple sage or nettle that Ruskin is puzzled to identify, and the chickweed green and rich and delicate. But if this seems enough to make his day, there are all the tomorrows of a new year, and an old habit of going to the fountain for guidance. As the first daybreak of January filters an orange glow behind the cloudbank, the Bible must be opened and the eye allowed to fall where it will—in this case at the thirtieth verse of the thirty-seventh chapter of Isaiah:

And this shall be the sign unto thee: ye shall eat this year that which groweth of itself, and in the second year that which springeth of the same; and in the third year sow ye, and reap, and plant vineyards, and eat the fruit thereof.

Good husbandry might lay the test to heart, but who could deduce from the oracle that little Rose La Touche was waiting around the corner? We are all nympholepts in running after our ideals, and none more so than John Ruskin, born under Aquarius.

For that matter, who could stake his credibility again upon a comet that had first tantalised the faithful and then cheated them? Yet in 1858 the night skies were to be streaked by it—or at least by *a* comet of unusual brilliance—in an anticlimactic display. The prophets and the table-rappers did their seasonal best at the turn of the year, and it was not beyond prediction that this time there would be something to bring Palmerston down. Yet the springs were hidden that would first restore him once again as Prime Minister, and then threaten him, on the threshold of his eightieth year, with a citation as co-respondent under the new Divorce Act. Nor could any clouded crystal ball offer a happier vision than that of his new Lord Chancellor, Lord Campbell, recommended to the office by the man he had crudely combated, Lord Lyndhurst; and welcomed to the Woolsack with a speech from him—"calm and clear as a deep pool upon rock," as Gladstone found Lyndhurst at eighty-six, but still with his keen perception of what is hollow and fantastical in human affairs. It was a speech that ended:

> Thou has it now—King, Cawdor, Glamis, all
> As the weird sisters promised.

Had the weird sisters been consulted about the Big Ship, they might have told Brunel what was wrong. For although he got her into the water at a later attempt, the *Great Eastern* broke his heart. Nothing went right for her, and only when she had at length been broken up was there found within her double bottom a human skeleton. With that information, any sailorman could have foretold her destiny.

"Thus ends the Indian Mutiny of 1857," proclaimed *The Times*. Wrong again. Lucknow had not been captured, Havelock was dead, and there were months of fighting and marching still to come.

> Ah, but my Computations, people say,
> Reduced the Year to better reckoning?—Nay,
> 'Twas only striking from the Calendar
> Unborn Tomorrow, and dead Yesterday.

FitzGerald had some idea of sending a few quatrains to *Frazer's Magazine*. "In truth," he wrote to Cowell, "I take old Omar rather more as my property than yours: he and I are more akin, are we not?" Ford Madox Brown wound up the year with work-statistics, Monckton Milnes with doggerel, George Eliot with thankfulness. Brown's calculation was of 2,626 hours of work in 1857—between seven and eight hours a day, Sundays included, and Milnes committed these lines among others:

> Away! you terrible Year!
> Take Madeleine Smith for better for worse;
> Give Robson and Redpath the care of your purse;
> Choose, as your ferryman over the Styx,
> Captain Rogers who kill'd the lad by his kicks.
> . . . .
> Begone! you pitiless Year!
> You that are branded with the shame
> Of India's broken faith and name,
> You that have heaped that hideous store
> Of noble death in the well of Cawnpore.
> . . . .
> Make way!—let the stage be clear
> For another and happier Year.
> . . . .
> Welcome, Lord of the unborn Fate,
> Eighteen hundred and fifty-eight!

Lewes was accustomed to spend the week after Christmas with the family of an old friend, leaving Marian to see the year out with her journal. "So goodbye, dear 1857!"

> My life has deepened unspeakably during the last year: I feel a greater capacity for moral and intellectual enjoyment, a more acute sense of my deficiencies in the past, a more solemn desire to be faithful to my coming duties, than I can remember at any former period of my life. And my happiness has deepened too: the blessedness of a perfect love and union grows daily . . . Few women, I fear, have had such reasons as I have to think the long sad years of youth were worth living for the sake of middle age.

So much for all the adolescent fire, the lives consumed before they are well begun, the vivid dreams peeling from the painted wall, the poems written only to be laid upon a corpse as pale as life, and only resting there until that impulse, too, is used up with the years. That the Wombat's Year is over is all too plain from the 1858 issue of Mr Mitchell's *Guide to the Zoological Society's Gardens*, where the hope is expressed that someone may soon present the Society with a koala bear. From the descriptions of zoologists, thinks Mr Mitchell, this rival attraction could not fail to capture public interest.

Whatever happens, Darwin will have the last word. "You ask," he wrote to Wallace at the end of December, "whether I shall discuss 'man.' I think I shall avoid the whole subject, as so surrounded with prejudices."